D0440863

"THIS BOOK

. . . is intended to spotlight commonly asked questions and to suggest at least preliminary answers.

For the strengthening of our own faith and for the help of others, we must be ready to give an answer to everyone who asks us for a reason for the hope that is within us, for Christianity is rational!"

While this book is designed for the reader's personal use and profit, it is also intended for group study. A leader's guide is available from your local bookstore or from the publisher at $1.25.

PAUL E. LITTLE

Until his death in July 1975, Paul E. Little was assistant to the president of the Inter-Varsity Christian Fellowship.

In addition to his activities with Inter-Varsity, Mr. Little served as associate professor of evangelism in the School of World Mission at Trinity Evangelical Divinity School, Deerfield, Illinois.

Mr. Little spoke on more than 200 campuses in the U.S., Canada, Latin America, Europe, and Africa. He pioneered Inter-Varsity's evangelistic beach activity during Easter vacation in Ft. Lauderdale, Florida. His best selling books, *How To Give Away Your Faith* and *Know Why You Believe,* have been translated into several languages. His latest book is *Know What You Believe.* Mr. Little served as a weekly columnist for the *Sunday School Times* and *Power Life.* His articles have appeared in *Eternity, Moody Monthly, Decision, HIS,* and other leading religious periodicals.

In 1957–58 Mr. Little spent seven months with the Billy Graham Evangelistic Association heading up the student phase of the New York and San Francisco Crusades. The program developed then set the pattern for the outreach to college and university students in succeeding crusades.

A graduate of the Wharton School of Finance of the University of Pennsylvania, Mr. Little also held the M.A. degree in Biblical Literature from Wheaton College and did graduate work at Chicago Lutheran Seminary.

KNOW
WHY
YOU
BELIEVE

Paul E. Little

VICTOR BOOKS

a division of SP Publications, Inc., Wheaton, Illinois
Offices also in Fullerton, California • Whitby, Ontario, Canada • London, England

Sixteenth printing, 1978

KNOW WHY YOU BELIEVE

Published for Victor Books, a Division of
SP Publications, Inc., by Pillar Books

ISBN: 0-88207-022-3

Library of Congress Catalog Card Number: 67-12231
Copyright © 1967, world rights reserved,
Scripture Press Publications, Inc., a wholly owned subsidiary
of Scripture Press Ministries

Printed in the United States of America

PREFACE
to the Second Edition

In a day when the foundations of our Christian faith are being assailed by seminary professors and by men in the pulpits of so-called Christian churches, this book reminds believers and convinces non-Christians that the affirmations of the Bible—and of historic Protestant Christianity— are *reasonable*. Considering how concise his volume is, Mr. Little has done a remarkable job of proving that an intelligent person need not apologize for accepting these teachings. Any teen-ager or adult who studies *Know Why You Believe* will be able to give *several* reasons (cf. I Pet. 3:15) for the hope that is in him! And most people, as they read Mr. Little's comments on some particular truth, will find themselves saying at least once, "What a good way to explain *that!*"

A glance at the chapter headings is enough to show you what a treat is in store for you as you read, and the author's easy writing style makes his book a delight.

The writer uses a wide range of research sources. His objective is to adduce the strongest possible support for the Christian teachings with which he deals. He draws on men who are abundantly qualified in the scientific subjects under discussion, and

he establishes the satisfying harmony between revealed truth and scientific truth.

Earlier printings of *Know Why You Believe*
have been widely acclaimed, and the book has already won a permanent place in the field of Christian Evidences. We are confident that this new edition will bring assurance to many readers.

THE EDITORS

CONTENTS

ACKNOWLEDGMENTS

The publisher and the author gratefully acknowledge the permission granted by a number of publishers for the use of quotations from copyright material, viz., The Macmillan Company, New York, for quotations from *God Our Contemporary*, by J. B. Phillips; the New American Library of World Literature, New York, for a quotation from *The Limitations of Science*, by J. W. N. Sullivan; E. P. Dutton & Co., Inc., New York, for a quotation from *Science Is a Sacred Cow*, by Anthony Standen; the Pergamon Press, New York, for a quotation from "Implications of Evolution," by G. A. Kerkut, in the *International Series of Monographs on Pure and Applied Biology*, Vol. 4; Farrar, Straus, & Giroux, Inc., New York, for a quotation from *Rivers in the Desert*, by Nelson Glueck; Encyclopaedia Britannica, Chicago, for a quotation from *Great Books of the Western World*, Vol. II, edited by Mortimer Adler; Inter-Varsity Christian Fellowship, Chicago, for a quotation from an article, "The Place of Reason," by John Montgomery in *His*, March, 1966, and for quotations from *The Mystery of Suffering*, by Hugh Evan Hopkins, from *Conversions: Psychological and Spiritual*, by D. Martyn Lloyd-Jones, and from *Basic Christianity*, by John R. W. Stott; Baker Book House Grand Rapids, for quotations from *Revelation and the Bible*, edited by Carl F. H. Henry; Wm. B. Eerdmans Publishing Co., Grand Rapids, for quotations from *The Christian View of Science and Scripture*, by Bernard Ramm, from *An Introduction to Christian Apologetics*, by E. J. Carnell, and from *The New Testament Documents: Are They Reliable?* by F. F. Bruce; to Inter-Varsity Fellowship and Tyndale Press, London, for quotations from *Creation*, by R. E. D. Clark, from *Questions of Science and Faith*, by J. N. Hawthorne, and from *Christianity in a Mechanistic Universe*, edited by D. M. MacKay; and to Moody Press, Chicago, for quotations from *Protestant Christian Evidences*, by Bernard Ramm, *The Bible and Modern Science*, by Henry Morris, *An Introduction to Bible Archaeology* and *Genesis and Archaeology*, by Howard F. Vos, and *Can I Trust My Bible?*

CHAPTER 1

IS CHRISTIANITY RATIONAL?

"WHAT IS FAITH?" asked the Sunday School teacher. A young boy answered in a flash, "Believing something you know isn't true."

That many non-Christians feel this way is not surprising. That many believers overtly or secretly feel this way is tragic.

Frequently I have the opportunity to present the Gospel in a bull session format. After a presentation, we have questions from the floor. Following these discussions I am often gratified and often dismayed. Unbelievers say the session has been helpful because it's the *first time* they've heard something that makes sense. I'm also gratified, but more deeply dismayed, when Christians tell me the same thing! They're relieved to discover that the Gospel can be successfully defended in the open marketplace of ideas and to discover they haven't kissed their brains good-bye in becoming Christians!

We live in an increasingly sophisticated and educated world. It is no longer enough to know *what* we believe. It is essential to know *why* we believe it. Believing something doesn't make it true. A

11

thing is true or not regardless of whether anyone believes it. This is as true of Christianity as of everything else.

There are two equally erroneous viewpoints abroad among Christians today on the important question of whether Christianity is rational. The first is, in essence, an anti-intellectual approach to Christianity. Many misunderstood verses like Colossians 2:8: "Beware lest anyone spoil you through philosophy or vain deceit, after the traditions of men, after the rudiments of the world and not after Christ." Some use this verse in a way that gives the impression that Christianity is at least non-rational if not irrational. They fail to realize that a clearly reasoned presentation of the Gospel "is important—not as a rational substitute for faith, but as a *ground* for faith; not as a replacement for the Spirit's working but as a means by which the objective truth of God's Word can be made clear so that men will heed it as the vehicle of the Spirit, who convicts the world through its message."[1]

There are challengers to our faith on every hand. Modern communications have made the world a neighborhood. We are likely to be challenged by Muslims, Hindus, and Buddhists, all of them claiming valid religious experience that may approximate ours. From within Christendom we are now being told God is dead. Increasingly, in our scientific age, ethical humanism is having stronger appeal. Julian Huxley's *Religion Without Revelation* is a good example of this approach.

Montgomery further observes, "The analytical philosopher, Anthony Flew, in developing a parable

---

[1]*Montgomery, J. W. "The Place of Reason,"* His, March 1966, p. 16.

from a tale told by John Wisdom, illustrates how meaningless to the non-Christian are religious assertions incapable of being tested objectively.

" 'Once upon a time two explorers came upon a clearing in the jungle. In the clearing were growing many flowers and many weeds. One explorer says, "Some gardener must tend this plot." The other disagrees, "There is no gardener." So they pitch their tents and set a watch. No gardener is ever seen. "But perhaps he is an invisible gardener." So they set up a barbed wire fence. They electrify it. They patrol with bloodhounds. (For they remember how H. G. Wells' *The Invisible Man* could be both smelt and touched though he could not be seen.) But no shrieks ever suggest that some intruder has received a shock. No movements of the wire ever betray an invisible climber. The bloodhounds never give cry. Yet still the believer is not convinced. "But there is a gardener, invisible, insensible to electric shocks, a gardener who comes secretly to look after the garden which he loves." At last the skeptic despairs, "But what remains of your original assertion? Just how does what you call an invisible, intangible, eternally elusive gardener differ from an imaginary gardener or even from no gardner at all?' "[2]

"This parable is a damning judgment on all religious truth-claims save that of the Christian faith.[3] For in Christianity we do not have merely an allegation that the garden of this world is tended by a loving Gardener; we have the actual, empirical en-

[2]*Flew, Anthony. "Theology and Falsification," New Essays* in Philosophical Theology, *ed. Flew and Macintyre. London: SCM Press, 1955.*

[3]*On the issue of theological verification, cf. Montgomery, "Inspiration and Inerrancy: a New Departure,"* Evangelical Theological Society Bulletin, *VIII (Spring 1965), pp. 45–75.*

trance of the Gardener into the human scene in the person of Christ (cf. John 20: 14, 15), and this entrance is verifiable by way of His resurrection."

On the other hand, there are those who naively trust a set of answers and try to argue people into the Kingdom. This is an impossibility and is as doomed to failure as attempting to put a hole in a brick wall by shooting it with a water pistol! There is an intellectual factor in the Gospel, but there are also moral considerations. "The natural man receiveth not the things of the Spirit of God: for they are foolishness unto him: neither can he know them, because they are spiritually discerned" (I Cor. 2:14). Apart from the work of the Holy Spirit, no man will believe. But one of the instruments the Holy Spirit uses to bring enlightenment is a reasonable explanation of the Gospel and of God's dealings with men.

Beyond these pragmatic considerations, however, are the Biblical assertions of the reasonableness of the Gospel. Along with this there are clear Biblical commands to Christians to be intelligent in their faith: "Be ready always to give an answer to every man that asketh you a reason of the hope that is in you, with meekness and fear" (I Pet. 3:15). If we are unable to give reasons for our faith, and if we allow the same questions to defeat us in conversation time after time, we are being disobedient. By our own ignorance, we are confirming unbelievers in their unbelief.

There are sound practical reasons why this command has been given us. In the first place, it is necessary for the strengthening of our faith as Christians. If we know Jesus lives only because, as the hymn says, "He lives within my heart," we're going to be in trouble the first time we don't feel He's there. And when someone from a non-Christian position claims to have experienced the same thing from *his* god, our mouths will be stopped. We may choose to ignore doubts, but eventually they will "get to us." One cannot indefinitely drive himself to do by willpower that of which he is not intellectually convinced. Witnessing, for example. He eventually suffers emotional collapse. When someone tells us the only reason we believe is because of our parents and our religious background, we must be able to show ourselves and others that what we believe is *objectively true*, regardless of who told us.

Many non-Christians fail to consider the Gospel seriously because no one has ever presented the facts to them cogently. They associate faith with superstition based primarily on emotional considerations, and therefore they reject it out of hand.

Further Biblical indication of the rational basis of the Gospel appears in our Lord's command to "love the Lord thy God with all thy heart and with all thy mind" (Matt. 22:37). The whole man is involved in conversion—the mind, the emotions, and the will. Paul says that he is "set for the defense of the Gospel" (Phil. 1:17). All of this implies a clearly understandable Gospel which can be rationally understood and defended.

It is quite true that an unenlightened mind cannot come to the truth of God unaided, but enlightenment brings comprehension of a *rational body of truth*.

The Gospel is always equated with truth. Truth is always the opposite of error (II Thess. 2:11, 12). Non-Christians are defined by Paul as those that "do not obey the truth" (Rom. 2:8). These statements would be meaningless unless there were a way to establish objectively what the truth is. If there were no such possibility, truth and error

15

would, for all practical purposes, be the same because we would have no way to tell one from the other.

In writing to the Romans, Paul makes it clear that men have enough knowledge from creation itself to know there is a God (Rom. 1:20). He goes on to show that the basic reason men do not know God is not because He cannot be known or understood but because men have rebelled against Him, their Creator. "When they knew God, they glorified Him not as God" (1:21), "changed the glory of the uncorruptible God into an image made like to corruptible man" (1:23), "changed the truth of God into a lie" (1:25), and, finally, "did not like to retain God in their knowledge" (1:28).

The moral issue always overshadows the intellectual issue in Christianity. It is not that man *cannot* believe—it is that he "*will* not believe." Jesus pointed the Pharisees to this as the root of the problem. "Ye *will* not come to me," He told them, "that ye might have life" (John 5:40). He makes it abundantly clear that moral commitment leads to a solution of the intellectual problem. "If any man *will* [wants to] do His will, he shall *know* of the doctrine, whether it be of God or whether I speak of myself" (John 7:17). Alleged intellectual problems are often a smoke screen covering moral rebellion.

A student once told me I had satisfactorily answered all his questions. "Are you going to become a Christian?" I asked. "No," he replied. Puzzled, I asked, "Why not?" He admitted, "Frankly, because it would mess up the way I'm living." He realized that the real issue for him was not intellectual but moral.

The question is often asked, "If Christianity is rational and true, why is it that most educated people don't believe it?" The answer is simple. They don't believe it for the very same reason that most *un*educated people don't believe it. They don't *want* to believe it. It's not a matter of brain power, for there are outstanding Christians in every field of the arts and sciences. It is primarily a matter of the will.

John Stott struck a balance when he said, "We cannot pander to a man's intellectual arrogance, but we must cater to his intellectual integrity."

Many Christians become troubled when they think about their faith and sometimes even wonder if it's true. Doubt is a word that strikes terror to the soul and often it is suppressed in a way that is very unhealthy. This is a particularly acute problem for those who have been reared in Christian homes and in the Christian Church. From their earliest years they have accepted the facts of Christianity solely on the basis of confidence and trust in parents, friends, and minister. As the educational process develops, a re-examination of their position takes place. This is a healthy and necessary experience to bring virile faith into being. It's nothing to fear or to be shocked about. Occasionally I ask myself, as I walk down the street, "Little, how do you know you haven't been taken in by a colossal propaganda program? After all, you can't see God, touch Him, taste Him or feel Him." And then I go on to ask myself how I *know* the Gospel is true. I always come back to two basic factors: the objective, external, historical facts of the Resurrection, and the subjective, internal, personal experience of Christ that I have known.

When young people begin to think and seem to have doubts, they should be welcomed into a climate where they are free to "unload" and *express* their doubts. Many such young people have been

17

driven underground and lost for good to the cause of Christ because the adults with whom they first talked had a high shock index. They implied that a good Christian would never doubt and that the questioner's spiritual life must be slipping because he was thinking. Young people aren't stupid. When they meet this response they quickly shift gears and mouth the party line, even though it doesn't come from the heart. They quietly wait until they are out from under pressure to conform, and then they shed a faith that had never become their very own.

Doubt and questioning are normal to any thinking person. Rather than express shock, it is better for us to hear the questioner out and, if possible, even sharpen the question a little more. Then an answer can be suggested. Because Christianity is about the One who is Truth, close examination can do it no harm.

If we don't have the answer at the moment, we needn't hit the panic button. We can always suggest we'll be glad to *get* the answer. It is improbable that anyone thought up, last week, the question that will bring Christianity crashing down. Brilliant minds have thought through the profound questions of every age and have ably answered them.

We don't have full answers to every question because the Lord hasn't fully revealed His mind to us on everything. "The secret things belong unto the Lord our God; but those things which are revealed belong unto us and to our children forever" (Deut. 29:29). We possess enough information, however, to have a solid foundation under our faith. Faith in Christianity is based on evidence. It is reasonable faith. Faith in the Christian sense goes beyond reason but not against it.

Despite these facts, many Christians are overwhelmed by a mountain of material which they erroneously think they must master if they are ever to answer the questions of thinking Christians and non-Christians. A little exposure to non-Christians, however, will help to dispel those fears. It will soon become apparent that the same few questions are being asked repeatedly. Further, these questions fall within a remarkably limited range. I frequently talk to audiences that are composed of 98 percent non-Christians. I can predict with a high degree of accuracy the questions that will be asked me in the course of a half-hour question period. The questions may vary in wording, but the underlying issues are the same. This consistency is a great help in knowing what to study to answer such questions.

A doubter needs to see that he must come to a decision after having been given an answer. To make no decision is to decide against the Christian position. Continued doubt in the face of adequate information may be a cloak for unwillingness to believe, in which case the problem is that the questioner's will has been set against God.

Recently, a friend told of a time, after he had finished college, when he felt God was calling him to the mission field. He fought against the call by feigning intellectual problems concerning his faith rather than by praying clearly about his unwillingness to go overseas.

This book is intended to spotlight commonly asked questions and to suggest at least preliminary answers.

For the strengthening of our own faith and for the help of others, we must be ready to give an answer to everyone who asks us a reason for the hope that is within us, for *Christianity is rational!*

CHAPTER 2

IS THERE A GOD?

THERE IS IN HUMAN existence no more profound question demanding an answer. "Is there a god?" is the question that must be answered by every human being, and the answer is far-reaching in its implications.

Mortimer Adler in his essay on God, in the monumental *Great Ideas Syntopicon* says, "With the exception of certain mathematicians and physicists, all the authors of the 'Great Books' are represented in this chapter. In sheer quantity of references, as well as in variety, it is the largest chapter. The reason is obvious. More consequences for thought and action follow the affirmation or denial of God than from answering any other basic question." He goes on to spell out the practical implications: "The whole tenor of human life is affected by whether men regard themselves as supreme beings in the universe or acknowledge a super-human being whom they conceive of as an object of fear or love, a force to be defied or a Lord to be obeyed. Among those who acknowledge a divinity, it matters greatly whether the divine is represented merely by the concept of God—the object of philosophical speculation—or by the living God whom men worship in all the acts of piety which comprise the rituals of religion."[1]

We must be clear from the outset that it is not possible to "prove" God in the scientific method sense of the word. But it can be said with equal emphasis that you can't "prove" Napoleon by the scientific method. The reason lies in the nature of history itself, and in the limitations of the scientific method. In order for something to be "proved" by the scientific method, it must be repeatable. One cannot announce a new finding to the world on the basis of a single experiment. But history in its very nature is nonrepeatable. No one can "rerun" the beginning of the universe or bring Napoleon back or repeat the assassination of Lincoln or the crucifixion of Jesus Christ. But the fact that these events can't be "proved" by repetition does not disprove their reality as events.

There are many real things outside the scope of verification by the scientific method. The scientific method is useful only with measurable things. No one has ever seen three feet of love or two pounds of justice, but one would be foolish indeed to deny their reality. To insist that God be "proved" by the scientific method is like insisting that a telephone be used to measure radioactivity. It simply wasn't made for that.

What evidence is there for God? Is it very significant that recent anthropological research has indicated that among the farthest and most remote primitive peoples, today, there is a universal belief in God. And in the earliest histories and legends of peoples all around the world the original concept

---

[1]Adler, Mortimer, Volume 2, p. 561, Great Books of the Western World, ed. Robert Maynard Hutchins.

was of one God, who was the Creator. An original high God seems once to have been in their consciousness even in those societies which are today polytheistic. This research, in the last 50 years, has challenged the evolutionary concept of the development of religion, which had suggested that monotheism—the concept of one God—was the apex of a gradual development that began with polytheistic concepts. It is increasingly clear that the oldest traditions everywhere were of one supreme God.[2]

For our present purposes, however, it is enough to observe that the vast majority of humanity, at all times and in all places, has believed in some kind of God or gods. Though this fact is not conclusive proof, by any means, we should keep it in mind as we attempt to answer the big question.

Then there is the law of cause and effect to consider. No effect can be produced without a cause. We as human beings, and the universe itself, are effects which must have had a cause. We come eventually to an uncaused cause, who is God. Bertrand Russell makes an astounding statement in his *"Why I Am Not a Christian."* He says that when he was a child, "God" was given him as the answer to the many questions he raised about existence. In desperation, he asked, "Well, who created God?" When no answer was forthcoming, he says, "My entire faith collapsed"! But how foolish. God by definition is eternal and uncreated. Were God a created being, He would not and could not be God.

A further development of this line of thought has to do with the clearly observable order and design of the universe. No one would think a wrist watch could come into being without an intelligent

---

[2]*Zwemer, Samuel.* The Origin of Religion.

designer. How much more incredible is it to believe that the universe, in its infinite complexity, could have happened by chance? The human body, for instance, is an admittedly astounding and complex organism—a continual marvel of organization, design, and efficiency. So impressed was he with this that Albert Einstein, generally considered to be one of the great scientists of all time, said, "My religion consists of a humble admiration of the illimitable superior Spirit who reveals Himself in the slight details we are able to perceive with our frail and feeble minds. That deeply emotional conviction of the presence of a superior reasoning power, which is revealed in the incomprehensible universe, forms my idea of God."[3]

Evidences of this design are abundant. It is unlikely that a monkey in a print shop could set Lincoln's *Gettysburg Address* in type. If we found a copy of it we would conclude that an intelligent mind was the only possible explanation for the printing. It is likewise incredible that water, for instance, with all its qualities, could have just happened. Bernard Ramm, quoting L. J. Henderson, enumerates some of these properties:

"Water has a high specific heat. This means that chemical reactions within the (human) body will be kept rather stable. If water had a low specific heat we would 'boil over' with the least activity. If we raise the temperature of a solution by 10 degrees Centigrade we speed up the reaction by two. Without this particular property of water, life would hardly be possible. The ocean is the world's thermostat. It takes a large loss of heat for water to pass from liquid to ice, and for water to become steam quite an intake of energy is required. Hence

---

[3]*Barnett, Lincoln.* The Universe and Dr. Einstein, *p. 95.*

the ocean is a cushion against the heat of the sun and the freezing blast of the winter. Unless the temperatures of the earth's surface were modulated by the ocean and kept within certain limits, life would either be cooked to death or frozen to death.

"Water is the universal solvent. It dissolves acids, bases and salts. Chemically, it is relatively inert, providing a medium for reactions without partaking in them. In the bloodstream it holds in solution the minimum of 64 substances. Perhaps if we knew the actual number it would be a staggering figure. Any other solvent would be a pure sludge! Without the peculiar properties of water, life as we know it would be impossible."[4]

A. Rendle Short makes this observation about water: "It forms more than half the body weight of most animals and plants. It is not readily decomposed; it dissolves many substances; it makes dry substances cohere and become flexible; with salts in solution, it conducts electricity. This is a very important property in the animal body. Then alone, or almost alone, amongst fluids known to us, it reaches its greatest density when cooled, not at freezing point, but at 4 degrees Centigrade. This has two important consequences. One is that lakes and ponds freeze at the top, and not from the bottom upwards. Fish life thus has a chance of surviving a very hard winter. Another consequence is that by its expansion on freezing water disrupts the rocks (also, alas, our household water pipes), and thus breaks them down to form soil, carves out cliffs and valleys, and makes vegetation possible. Water has the highest heat of evaporation of any

[4]*Ramm, Bernard.* The Christian View of Science and Scripture, *p. 148. Grand Rapids: Wm. B. Eerdmans, 1955.*

known substance. This, with other special properties, reduces the rise in temperature when a water surface is heated by the sun's rays."[5]

The earth itself is evidence of design. "If it were much smaller an atmosphere would be impossible (e.g., Mercury and the moon); if much larger the atmosphere would contain free hydrogen (e.g., Jupiter and Saturn). Its distance from the sun is correct—even a small change would make it too hot or too cold. Our moon, probably responsible for the continents and ocean basins, is unique in our solar system and seems to have originated in a way quite different from the other relatively much smaller moons. The tilt of the [earth's] axis insures the seasons, and so on."[6]

DuNoüy says that "the chance formulations of a typical protein molecule made up of 3,000 atoms is of the order of one of 2.02×10^{231}, or practically nil. Even if the elements are shaken up at the speed of the vibration of light, it would take 10^{234} billions of years to get the protein molecule [needed] for life, and life on the earth is limited to about two billion years."[7]

In addition to design in the universe, there is the implication of the second law of thermodynamics, which is also called the law of entropy. Ramm explains it: "What the law asserts can be illustrated from a plastic oleomargarine bag which contains white margarine and a small capsule filled with yellow coloring. When the capsule is broken, as the bag is massaged, the coloring is eventually spread

[5]*Short, A. Rendle.* Modern Discovery and the Bible, p. 39. London: Inter-Varsity Christian Fellowship, 1949.
[6]*Clark, R. E. D.* Creation, p. 20. London: Tyndale Press, 1946.
[7]*Ramm.* Op. cit., p. 148.

throughout the mass of white margarine. If the bag is squeezed indefinitely the distribution of the coloring will proceed till the coloring is perfectly spread throughout the entire mass. No matter how much more we squeeze, we cannot reverse the process and get the coloring back into the capsule. There are some parts of the universe that are much hotter than other parts of the universe. The distribution of the heat is always 'down' from hotter regions to cooler regions. As the heat 'flows' from the hot regions to cooler regions, it becomes more and more evenly distributed throughout the universe. If the universe is infinitely old, the energy would have been evenly distributed by now. The fact that there are still hot bodies in the universe means that the furnace was stoked, so to speak, at some measurable time in the past. This would be the moment of creation, or of some creative activity."[8]

In the light of all these things we can conclude with Ramm's statement: "Genesis 1 now stands in higher repute than it could ever have stood in the history of science up to this point. We now have means whereby we can point to a moment of time, or to an event or cluster of events in time, which dates our present known universe. According to the best available data, that is of the order of four to five billion years ago. A series of calculations converge on about the same order of time. We cannot with our present information force a verdict for creation from the scientists, though that is not to be considered an impossibility. Perhaps the day will come when we have enough evidence from physics, astronomy, and astrophysics to get such a verdict from the scientists. In the meantime we can

---

[8]*Ramm. Op. cit., p. 154.*

maintain that Genesis 1 is not out of harmony with the trend of scientific information."[9]

This is what the Apostle Paul had in mind when he wrote, "Because that which may be known of God is manifest in them; for God hath showed it unto them. For the invisible things of Him from the creation of the world are clearly seen, being understood by the things that are made, even His eternal power and Godhead; so that they are without excuse" (Rom. 1:19, 20). The psalmist says the same thing: "The heavens declare the glory of God; and the firmament showeth His handiwork" (Ps. 19:1).

But prejudice often prevents the most obvious conclusions. A most remarkable admission of unscientific bias, which precludes an admission that God is the only plausible explanation of the origin of the universe, is made by J. W. N. Sullivan. At his death, *Time* called him "one of the world's four or five most brilliant interpreters of physics to the world of common man." He said: "The beginning of the evolutionary process raises a question which is as yet unanswerable. What was the origin of life on this planet? Until fairly recent times there was a pretty general belief in the occurrence of 'spontaneous generation.' It was supposed that lowly forms of life developed spontaneously from, for example, putrefying meat. But careful experiments, notably those of Pasteur, showed that this conclusion was due to improper observation, and it became an accepted doctrine that life never arises except from life. So far as actual evidence goes, this is still the only possible conclusion. But since it is a conclusion that seems to lead back to some supernatural creative act, it is a conclusion that scientif-

---

[9]*Ramm*. Op. cit., *p. 154.*

ic men find very difficult to accept. It carries with it what are felt to be, in the present mental climate, undesirable philosophic implications, and it is opposed to the scientific desire for continuity. It introduces an unaccountable break in the chain of causation, and therefore cannot be admitted as part of science unless it is quite impossible to reject it. For that reason most scientific men prefer to believe that life arose, in some way not yet understood, from inorganic matter in accordance with the laws of physics and chemistry."[10]

Here we have an example of how believing there is *no* God is also an act of faith. It is pure presupposition, as much as faith *in* God is a presupposition for belief. Unbelief is even more remarkable when it is admitted that the evidence, by which one is guided in science, points in the opposite direction! And science rejects the conclusion because it is an unpalatable one.

It is important to observe here that though there are many *indications* of God in nature, we could never know conclusively from nature that He *is* or what He is *like*. The question asked centuries ago, "Canst thou by searching find out God" (Job 11:7). The answer is NO! Unless God reveals Himself, we are doomed to confusion and conjecture.

It is obvious that among those who believe in God there are many ideas abroad today as to what God is like. Some, for instance, believe God to be a celestial killjoy. They view Him as peering over the balcony of heaven looking for anyone who seems to be enjoying life. On finding such a person, He shouts down, "Cut it out!"

Others think of God as a sentimental grandfa-

---
[10]*Sullivan, J. W. N.* The Limitations of Science, *p. 94. New York: New American Library, 1956.*

ther of the sky, rocking benignly and stroking His beard as He says, "Boys will be boys!" That everything will work out in the end, no matter what you have done, is conceded to be His general attitude toward man. Others think of Him as a big ball of fire and of us as little sparks who will eventually come back to the big ball. Still others, like Einstein, think of God as an impersonal force or mind. Herbert Spencer, one of the popularizers of agnosticism of a century ago, observed accurately that a bird has never been known to fly out of space. Therefore he concluded by analogy that it is impossible for the finite to penetrate the infinite. His observation was correct, but his conclusion was wrong. He missed one other possibility: that the infinite could penetrate the finite. This, of course, is what God has done.

As the writer to the Hebrews puts it, "God, who at sundry times and in divers manners spake in time past unto the fathers by the prophets, hath in these last days spoken unto us by His Son" (Heb. 1:1, 2).

God has taken the initiative, throughout history, to communicate to man. His fullest revelation has been His invasion into human history in the person of Jesus Christ. Here, in terms of human personality that we can understand, He has lived among us. If you wanted to communicate your love to a colony of ants, how could you most effectively do it? Clearly, it would be best to become an ant. Only in this way could your existence and what you were like be communicated fully and effectively. This is what God did with us. We are, as J. B. Phillips aptly put it, "the visited planet." The best and clearest answer to how we know there is a God is that He has visited us. The other indications are merely clues or hints. What confirms them conclusively is the birth, life, death, and resurrection of Jesus Christ.

Other evidence for the reality of God's existence is His Clear presence in the lives of men and women today. Where Jesus Christ is believed and trusted a profound change takes place in the individual—and ultimately the community. One of the most moving illustrations of this is recorded by Ernest Gordon, now chaplain at Princeton University. In his *Valley of the Kwai* he tells how, during World War II, the prisoners of the Japanese on the Malay peninsula had been reduced almost to animals, stealing food from their buddies, who were also starving. In their desperation the prisoners decided it would be good to read the New Testament.

Because Gordon was a university graduate, they asked him to lead. By his own admission, he was a skeptic—and those who asked him to lead them were unbelievers, too. He and others came to trust Christ on becoming acquainted with Him in all of His beauty and power through the uncluttered simplicity of the New Testament. How this group of scrounging, clawing humans was transformed into a community of love is a touching and powerful story that demonstrates clearly the reality of God in Jesus Christ. Many others today, in less dramatic terms, have experienced this same reality.

There is, then, evidence from creation, history, and contemporary life that there is a God and that this God can be known in personal experience.

CHAPTER 3

IS CHRIST GOD?

IT IS IMPOSSIBLE for us to know conclusively whether God exists and what He is like unless He takes the initiative and reveals Himself. We must know what He is like and His attitude toward us. Suppose we knew He existed, but that He was like Adolf Hitler—capricious, vicious, prejudiced, and cruel. What a horrible realization that would be!

We must scan the horizon of history to see if there is any clue to God's revelation. There is one clear clue. In an obscure village in Palestine, almost 2,000 years ago, a child was born in a stable. His birth was feared by the reigning monarch, Herod. In an attempt to destroy this baby, who was said to be the King of the Jews, Herod had many infants killed in what history knows as the "slaughter of the innocents."

The baby and His parents settled in Nazareth, where Jesus learned His father's trade of carpentry. He was an unusual child. When He was 12 years old He confounded the scholars and rabbis in Jerusalem. When His parents remonstrated with Him because He had stayed behind after they departed, He made the strange reply, "Don't you realize I must be about My Father's business?" This answer implied a unique relationship between Him and God.

He lived in obscurity until He was 30, and then began a public ministry that lasted for three years. It was destined to change the course of history.

He was a kindly person and we're told that "the common people heard Him gladly." Unlike the religious teachers of His time, "He spoke with authority, and not as the scribes and Pharisees."

It soon became apparent, however, that He was making shocking and startling statements about Himself. He began to identify Himself as far more than a remarkable teacher or a prophet. He began to say clearly that He was Deity. He made His identity the focal point of His teaching. The all-important question He put to those who followed Him was, "Whom do you say that I, the Son of Man, am?" When Peter answered and said, "Thou art the Christ, the Son of the living God" (Matt. 16:15, 16), He was not shocked, nor did He rebuke Peter. On the contrary, He commended him!

He made the claim explicitly, and His hearers got the full impact of His words. We are told, "Therefore the Jews sought the more to kill Him, because He not only had broken the Sabbath but said also that God was His Father, making Himself equal with God" (John 5:18).

On another occasion, He said, "I and My Father are one." Immediately the Jews wanted to stone Him. He asked them for which good work they wanted to kill Him. They replied, "For a good work we stone Thee not; but for blasphemy and because that Thou, being a man, makest Thyself God" (John 10:30-33).

Jesus clearly claimed attributes which only God has. When a paralytic was let down through a roof and placed at His feet, He said, "Son, thy sins be forgiven thee." This caused a great to-do among the scribes, who said in their hearts, "Why does this man thus speak blasphemies? Who can forgive sins but God only?" Jesus, knowing their thoughts, said to them, "Whether it is easier, to say to the sick of the palsy, 'Thy sins be forgiven thee,' or to say, 'Arise, and take up thy bed and walk'?" Then He said, in effect, "But that you may know that I, the Son of Man, have power on earth to forgive sins [which you rightly say God alone can do, but which is invisible], I'll do something you can *see*." Turning to the palsied man, He commanded him, "Arise, and take up thy bed, and go thy way unto thine house" (Luke 2:7-11).

That the title "Son of Man" is an assertion of deity, rather than being a disclaimer of it as some have suggested, is seen in the attributes Jesus claims as Son of Man. These obviously are true only of God.

At the critical moment when His life was at stake because of this claim, He asserted it to the high priest, who had put the question to Him directly: "Art Thou the Christ, the Son of the blessed?" He said, "I am." Then He continued, "And ye shall see the Son of Man sitting on the right hand of power and coming in the clouds of Heaven." The high priest tore his clothes and said, "What need we of any further witnesses? Ye have heard the blasphemy" (Mark 14:61-64).

"So close was His connection with God that He equated a man's attitude to Himself with the man's attitude to God. Thus, to know Him was to know God (John 8:19; 14:7). To see Him was to see God (12:45; 14:9). To believe in Him was to believe in God (12:44; 14:1). To receive Him was to receive God (Mark 9:37). To hate Him was

33

to hate God (John 15:23). And to honor Him was to honor God (5:23)."[1]

As we face the claims of Christ, there are only four possibilities. He was either a liar, a lunatic, a legend, or the Truth. If we say He is not the Truth, we are automatically affirming one of the other three alternatives, whether we realize it or not. When friends of ours take this position, we should invite them to show us what evidence they have that would lead us to adopt it. Often they realize, for the first time, that there is no evidence to support their views. Rather, all the evidence points in the other direction.

One possibility is that Jesus Christ lied when He said He was God—that He knew He was not God, but deliberately deceived His hearers to lend authority to His teaching. Few, if any, seriously hold this position. Even those who deny His deity affirm that they think Jesus was a great moral teacher. They fail to realize those two statements are a contradiction. Jesus could hardly be a great moral teacher if, on the most crucial point of His teaching, i.e., His identity, He was a deliberate liar.

A kinder, though no less shocking possibility, is that He was sincere but self-deceived. We have a name for a person today who thinks he is God—or a poached egg! That name is *lunatic*, and it certainly would apply to Christ if He were deceived on this all-important issue.

But as we look at the life of Christ, we see no evidence of the abnormality and imbalance we find in a deranged person. Rather, we find the greatest composure under pressure. At His trial before Pilate, when His very life was at stake, He was calm

[1]Stott, John R. W. Basic Christianity, p. 26. Chicago: Inter-Varsity Press, 1964.

and serene. As C. S. Lewis put it, "The discrepancy between the depth and sanity of His moral teaching and the rampant megalomania which must lie behind His theological teaching unless He is indeed God has never been satisfactorily got over."[2]

The third alternative is that all of the talk about His claiming to be God is a legend—that what actually happened was that His enthusiastic followers, in the third and fourth centuries, put words into His mouth He would have been shocked to hear. Were He to return He would immediately repudiate them.

The problem with the legend theory is the discoveries of modern archaeology. It has been conclusively shown that the four biographies of Christ were written within the lifetime of contemporaries of Christ. Some time ago Dr. William F. Albright, world-famous archaeologist, now retired from Johns Hopkins University, said that there was no reason to believe that any of the Gospels were written later than A.D. 70. For a mere legend about Christ, in the form of the Gospel, to have gained the circulation and to have had the impact it had, without one shred of basis in fact, is incredible. For this to have happened would be as fantastic as for someone in our own time to write a biography of the late Franklin Delano Roosevelt and in it say he claimed to be God, to forgive people's sins, and to have risen from the dead. Such a story is so wild it would never get off the ground because there are still too many people around who knew Roosevelt! The legend theory does not hold water in the light of the early date of the Gospel manuscripts.

---

[2]*Stott.* Ibid., *p. 32, quoting C. S. Lewis,* Miracles.

The only other alternative is that Jesus spoke the truth.

From one point of view, however, claims don't mean much. Talk is cheap. Anyone can make claims. There have been others who have claimed deity. A recent one was Father Divine, of Philadelphia, now deceased. I could claim to be God, and you could claim to be God, but the question all of us must answer is, What credentials do we bring to substantiate our claim? In my case it wouldn't take you five minutes to disprove my claim. It probably wouldn't take too much more to dispose of yours. It certainly wasn't difficult to show that Father Divine was not God. But when it comes to Jesus of Nazareth, it's not so simple. He had the credentials to back up His claim. He said, "Though ye believe not Me, believe [My] works that ye may know and believe that the Father is in Me and I in Him" (John 10:38).

What were His credentials?

First, His character coincided with His claims. We saw earlier that many asylum inmates claim to be various people. But their claims are belied by their character. Not so with Christ. And we do not *compare* Christ with others— we *contrast* Him with all others. He is unique—as unique as God.

Jesus Christ was sinless. The caliber of His life was such that He was able to challenge His enemies with the question, "Which of you convinceth Me of sin?" (John 8:46). He was met by silence, even though He addressed those who would have liked to point out a flaw in His character.

We read of the temptations of Jesus, but we never hear of a confession of sin on His part. He never asks for forgiveness, though He tells His followers to do so.

This lack of any sense of moral failure on Jesus'

part is astonishing in view of the fact that it is completely contrary to the experience of the saints and mystics in all ages. The closer men and women draw to God, the more overwhelmed they are with their own failure, corruption, and shortcoming. The closer one is to a shining light, the more he realizes his need of a bath. This is true also, in the moral realm, for ordinary mortals.

It is also striking that John, Paul, and Peter, all of whom were trained from earliest childhood to believe in the universality of sin, all speak of the sinlessness of Christ: "Who did no sin, neither was guile found in His mouth" (I Pet. 2:22); "In Him is no sin" (I John 3:5); Jesus "knew no sin" (II Cor. 5:21).

Pilate, no friend of Jesus, said, "What evil has He done?" He implicitly recognized Christ's innocence. And the Roman centurion who witnessed the death of Christ said, "Truly this was the Son of God" (Matt. 27:54).

In Jesus we find the perfect personality. Ramm points out, "If God were a man, we would expect His personality to be true humanity. Only God could tell us what a true man should be like. Certainly there are anticipations of the perfect man in the piety of the Old Testament. Foremost must be a complete God-consciousness, coupled with a complete dedication and consecration of life to God. Then, ranked below this, are the other virtues, graces, and attributes that characterize perfect humanity. Intelligence must not stifle piety, and prayer must not be a substitute for work, and zeal must not be irrational fanaticism, and reserve must not become stolidity. In Christ we have the perfect blend of personality traits, because as God Incarnate He is perfect humanity. Schaff describes our Lord, with reference to this point of our discussion, as follows: 'His zeal never degenerated into passion, nor His constancy into obstinacy, nor His benevolence into weakness, nor His tenderness into sentimentality. His unworldliness was free from indifference and unsociability or undue familiarity; His self-denial from moroseness; His temperance from austerity. He combined child-like innocency with manly strength, absorbing devotion to God with untiring interest in the welfare of man, tender love to the sinner with uncompromising severity against sin, commanding dignity with winning humility, fearless courage with wise caution, unyielding firmness with sweet gentleness!'[3]

Christ demonstrated a power over natural forces which could belong only to God, the Author of these forces.

He stilled a raging storm of wind and waves on the Sea of Galilee. In doing this He provoked from those in the boat the awestruck question, "What manner of man is this, that even the wind and the sea obey Him?" (Mark 4:41) He turned water into wine, fed 5,000 people from five loaves and two fish, gave a grieving widow back her only son by raising him from the dead, and brought to life the dead daughter of a shattered father. To an old friend He said, "Lazarus, come forth!" and dramatically raised him from the dead. It is most significant that His enemies did not deny this miracle. Rather, they tried to kill Him. "If we let Him thus alone," they said, "all men will believe on Him" (John 11:48).

Jesus demonstrated the Creator's power over sickness and disease. He made the lame to walk, the dumb to speak, and the blind to see. Some of

---

[3]*Ramm, Bernard.* Protestant Christian Evidences, *p. 177. Chicago: Moody Press, 1953.*

His healings were of congenital problems not susceptible to phychosomatic cure. The most outstanding was that of the blind man whose case is recorded in John 9. Though the man couldn't answer his speculative questioners, his experience was enough to convince *him*. "Whereas I was blind, now I see," he declared. He was astounded that his friends didn't recognize his Healer as the Son of God. "Since the world began was it not heard that any man opened the eyes of one that was born blind," he said. To him the evidence was obvious.

Jesus' supreme credential to authenticate His claim to deity was His resurrection from the dead. Five times in the course of His life He predicted He would die. He also predicted how He would die and that three days later He would rise from the dead and appear to His disciples.

Surely this was the great test. It was a claim that was easy to verify. It either happened or it didn't.

The Resurrection is so crucial and foundational a subject we will devote a whole chapter to it. If the Resurrection happened, there is no difficulty with any other miracles. And if we establish the Resurrection, we have the answer to the big question of God, His character, and our relationship to Him. An answer to this question makes possible answers to all subsidiary questions.

Christ moved history as only God could do. Schaff very graphically says, "This Jesus of Nazareth, without money and arms, conquered more millions than Alexander, Caesar, Muhammad, and Napoleon; without science and learning, He shed more light on matters human and divine than all philosophers and scholars combined; without the eloquence of schools, He spoke such words of life as were never spoken before or since and produced effects which lie beyond the reach of orator or poet; without writing a single line, He set more pens in motion, and furnished themes for more sermons, orations, discussions, learned volumes, works of art, and songs of praise than the whole army of great men of ancient and modern times."

Finally, we know that Christ is God because we can experience Him in the twentieth century. Experience in itself is not conclusive, but combined with the historic objective fact of the Resurrection it gives us the basis for our solid conviction. There is no other hypothesis to explain all the data we have than the profound fact that Jesus Christ is God the Son.

CHAPTER 4

DID CHRIST
RISE FROM THE DEAD?

BOTH FRIENDS and enemies of the Christian faith have recognized the resurrection of Christ to be the foundation stone of the Faith. Paul, the great apostle, wrote to those in Corinth, who in general denied the resurrection of the dead: "If Christ be not risen, then is our preaching vain, and your faith is also vain." Paul rested his whole case on the bodily resurrection of Christ. Either He did or He didn't rise from the dead. If He *did*, it was the most sensational event in all of history and we have conclusive answers to the profound questions of our existence: Where have we come from? Why are we here? Where are we going? If Christ rose, we know with certainty that God exists, what He is like, and how we may know Him in personal experience; the universe takes on meaning and purpose, and it is possible to experience the living God in contemporary life. These and many other wonderful things are true if Jesus of Nazareth rose from the dead.

On the other hand, if Christ did *not* rise from the dead, Christianity is an interesting museum piece—nothing more. It has no objective validity

41

or reality. Though it is a nice wishful thought, it certainly isn't worth getting steamed up about. The martyrs who went singing to the lions, and contemporary missionaries who have given their lives in Ecuador and Congo while taking this message to others, have been poor deluded fools.

The attack on Christianity by its enemies has most often concentrated on the Resurrection because it has been correctly seen that this event is the crux of the matter. A remarkable attack was the one contemplated in the early thirties by a young British lawyer. He was convinced that the Resurrection was a mere tissue of fable and fantasy. Sensing that it was the foundation stone of the Christian faith, he decided to do the world a favor by once-and-for-all exposing this fraud and superstition. As a lawyer, he felt he had the critical faculties rigidly to sift evidence and to admit nothing as evidence which did not meet the stiff criteria for admission into a law court today.

However, while he was doing his research, a remarkable thing happened. The case was not nearly as easy as he had supposed. As a result, the first chapter of his book is entitled, "The Book That Refused to Be Written." In it he describes how, as he examined the evidence, he became persuaded against his will, of the fact of the bodily resurrection.

The book is called, *Who Moved the Stone?* The author is Frank Morrison.

What are some of the pieces of data to be considered in answering the question, Did Christ rise from the dead?

First, there is the fact of the Christian Church. It is worldwide in scope. Its history can be traced back to Palestine around A.D. 32. Did it just happen or was there a cause for it? These people who were first called Christians at Antioch turned the world of their time upside down. They constantly referred to the Resurrection as the basis for their teaching, preaching, living, and—significantly—dying.

Then, there is the fact of the Christian Day. Sunday is the day of worship for Christians. Its history can also be traced back to the year A.D. 32. Such a shift in the calendar was monumental, and something cataclysmic must have happened to change the day of worship from the Jewish Sabbath, the seventh day of the week, to Sunday, the first day. Christians said the shift came because of their desire to celebrate the resurrection of Jesus from the dead. This shift is all the more remarkable when we remember that the first Christians were Jews. If the Resurrection does not account for this monumental upheaval, what does?

Then there is the Christian Book, the New Testament. In its pages are contained six independent testimonies to the fact of the Resurrection. Three of them are by eyewitnesses: John, Peter, and Matthew. Paul, writing to the churches at an early date, refers to the Resurrection in such a way that it is obvious to him and his readers that the event was well known and was accepted without question. Are these men, who helped transform the moral structure of society, consummate liars or deluded madmen? These alternatives are harder to believe than the fact of the Resurrection, and there is no shred of evidence to support them.

Two facts must be explained by believer and unbeliever alike. They are the empty tomb and the alleged appearances of Christ.

How can we account for the empty tomb?

The earliest explanation circulated was that the disciples stole the body. In Matthew 28:11-15, we have the record of the reaction of the chief priests and the elders when the guards gave them the infuriating and mysterious news that the body was gone. They gave the soldiers money and told them to explain that the disciples had come at night and stolen the body while they were asleep. That story is so obviously false that Matthew doesn't even bother to refute it! What judge would listen to you if you said that while you were asleep your neighbor came into your house and stole your television set? Who knows what goes on while he's asleep? Testimony like this would be laughed out of any court. Furthermore, we are faced with a psychological and ethical impossibility. Stealing the body of Christ is something totally foreign to the character of the disciples and all that we know of them. It would mean that they were perpetrators of a deliberate lie which was responsible for the misleading and ultimate death of thousands of people. It is inconceivable that, even if a few of the disciples had conspired and pulled off this theft, they would never have told the others.

Each of the disciples faced the test of torture and martyrdom for his statements and beliefs. Men will die for what they *believe* to be true, though it may actually be false. They do not, however, die for what they *know* is a lie. If ever a man tells the truth, it is on his deathbed. And if the disciples *had* taken the body, and Christ was still dead, we would still have the problem of explaining His alleged appearances.

A second hypothesis is that the authorities, Jewish or Roman, moved the body. But why? Having put guards at the tomb, what would be their reason for moving the body? But there is also a convincing answer for this thesis—the silence of the authorities in the face of the apostles' bold preaching about the Resurrection in Jerusalem. The ecclesiastical leaders were seething with rage, and did everything possible to prevent the spread of this message and to suppress it (Acts 4). They arrested Peter and John and beat and threatened them, in an attempt to close their mouths.

But there was a very simple solution to their problem. If they had Christ's body, they could have paraded it through the streets of Jerusalem. In one fell swoop they would have successfully smothered Christianity in its cradle. That they did not do this bears eloquent testimony to the fact that they did *not* have the body.

Another popular theory has been that the women, distraught and overcome by grief, missed their way in the dimness of the morning and went to the wrong tomb. In their distress they *imagined* Christ had risen because the tomb was empty. This theory, however, falls before the same fact that destroys the previous one. If the women went to the wrong tomb, why did the high priests and other enemies of the faith not go to the right tomb and produce the body? Further, it is inconceivable that Peter and John would succumb to the same mistake, and certainly Joseph of Arimathea, owner of the tomb, would have solved the problem. In addition, it must be remembered that this was a private burial ground, not a public cemetery. There was no other tomb there that would have allowed them to make this mistake.

The swoon theory has also been advanced to explain the empty tomb. In this view, Christ did not actually die. He was mistakenly reported to be dead, but had swooned from exhaustion, pain, and loss of blood. When He was laid in the coolness of the tomb, He revived. He came out of the tomb and appeared to his disciples, who mistakenly thought He had risen from the dead.

This is a theory of modern construction. It first appeared at the end of the eighteenth century. It is significant that not a suggestion of this kind has come down from antiquity among all the violent attacks which have been made on Christianity. All of the earliest records are emphatic about Jesus' *death*.

But let us assume for a moment that Christ was buried alive and swooned. Is it possible to believe that He would have survived three days in a damp tomb without food or water or attention of any kind? Would He have survived being wound in spice-laden grave clothes? Would He have had the strength to extricate Himself from the grave clothes, push the heavy stone away from the mouth of the grave, overcome the Roman guards, and walk miles on feet that had been pierced with spikes? Such a belief is more fantastic than the simple fact of the Resurrection itself.

Even the German critic, David Strauss, who by no means believes in the Resurrection, rejected this idea as incredible. He says, "It is impossible that One who had just come forth from the grave, half dead, who crept about weak and ill, who stood in the need of medical treatment, of bandaging, strengthening, and tender care, and who at last succumbed to suffering, could ever have given the disciples the impression that He was a conqueror over death and the grave; that He was the Prince of Life. This lay at the bottom of their future ministry. Such a resuscitation could only have weakened the impression which He had made upon them in life and in death—or at the most, could have given in an elegiac voice—but could by no possibility have changed their sorrow into enthusiasm or elevated their reverence into worship."[1]

Finally, if this theory is correct, Christ Himself was involved in flagrant lies. His disciples believed and preached that He was dead but became alive again. Jesus did nothing to dispel this belief, but rather encouraged it.

The only theory that adequately explains the empty tomb is the resurrection of Jesus Christ from the dead.

The second piece of data that everyone, whether believer or unbeliever, must explain is the recorded appearances of Christ. These occurred from the morning of His resurrection to His ascension 40 days later. Ten distinct appearances are recorded. They show great variety as to time, place, and people. Two were to individuals, Peter and James. There were appearances to the disciples as a group, and one was to 500 assembled brethren. The appearances were at different places. Some were in the garden near His tomb, some were in the upper room. One was on the road from Jerusalem to Emmaus, and some were far away, in Galilee. Each appearance was characterized by different acts and words by Jesus.

For the same reasons that the empty tomb cannot be explained on the basis of lies or legends, neither can we dismiss the statement of the appearances of Christ on this basis. This is testimony given by eyewitnesses fully and profoundly convinced of the truth of their statements.

The major theory advanced to explain away the accounts of the appearances of Christ is that they were hallucinations. At first, this sounds like a

[1]*Strauss, David.* The Life of Jesus for the People, *English trans., 2nd edition; I, p. 412. London, 1879.*

plausible explanation of an otherwise supernatural event. It is plausible until we begin to realize that modern medicine has observed that certain laws apply to such psychological phenomena. As we relate these principles to the evidence at hand, we see that what at first seemed most plausible is, in fact, impossible.

Hallucinations occur generally in people who tend to be vividly imaginative and of a nervous makeup. But the appearances of Christ were to all sorts of people. True, some were possibly emotional women, but there were also hardheaded men like the fisherman, Peter, and others of various dispositions.

Hallucinations are extremely subjective and individual. For this reason, no two people have the same experience. But in the case of the Resurrection, Christ appeared not just to individuals, but to *groups*, including one of more than 500 people. Paul says that more than half of them were still alive and could tell about these events (I Cor. 15).

Hallucinations usually occur only at particular times and places, and are associated with the events fancied. But these appearances occurred both indoors and outdoors, in the morning, afternoon, and evening.

Generally these psychic experiences occur over a long period of time with some regularity. But these experiences happened during a period of 40 days, and then stopped abruptly. No one ever said they happened again.

But perhaps the most conclusive indication of the fallacy of the hallucination theory is a fact often overlooked. In order to have an experience like this, one must so intensely *want* to believe that he projects something that really isn't there and attaches reality to his imagination. For instance, a mother who has lost a son in the war remembers how he used to come home from work every evening at 5:30 o'clock. She sits in her rocking chair every afternoon musing and meditating. Finally, she thinks she sees him come through the door, and has a conversation with him. At this point she has lost contact with reality.

One might think that this was what happened to the disciples about the Resurrection. The fact is that the opposite took place—they were persuaded *against their wills* that Jesus had risen from the dead!

Mary came to the tomb on the first Easter Sunday morning with spices in her hands. Why? To anoint the dead body of the Lord she loved. She was obviously not expecting to find Him risen from the dead. In fact, when she first saw Him she mistook Him for the gardener! It was only after He spoke to her and identified Himself that she realized who He was.

When the other disciples heard, they didn't believe. The story seemed to them "as an idle tale."

When the Lord finally appeared to the disciples, they were frightened and thought they were seeing a ghost! They thought they were having a hallucination, and it jolted them. He finally had to tell them, "Handle Me and see, for a spirit hath not flesh and bones as ye see Me have." He asked them if they had any food, and they gave Him a piece of broiled fish. Luke doesn't add the obvious—ghosts don't eat fish! (Luke 24:36-43)

Finally, there is the classic case of which we still speak—Thomas, the doubter. He was not present when the Lord appeared to the disciples the first time. They told him about it, but he scoffed and would not believe. In effect, he said, "I'm from Missouri. I won't believe unless I'm shown. I'm an empiricist. Unless I can put my finger into the nail wounds in His hands and my hand into His side, I will not believe." *He* wasn't about to have a hallucination!

John gives us the graphic story (John 20) of our Lord's appearance to the disciples eight days later. He graciously invited Thomas to examine the evidence of His hands and His side. Thomas looked at Him and fell down in worship: "My Lord and my God."

To hold the hallucination theory in explaining the appearances of Christ, one must completely ignore the evidence.

What was it that changed a band of frightened, cowardly disciples into men of courage and conviction? What was it that changed Peter from one who, the night before the Crucifixion, was so afraid for his own skin that he three times denied he even knew Jesus, into a roaring lion of the faith? Some 50 days later Peter risked his life by saying he had seen Jesus risen from the dead. It must be remembered that Peter preached his electric Pentecost sermon in Jerusalem, where the events took place and his life was in danger. He was not in Galilee, miles away, where no one could verify the facts and where his ringing statements might go unchallenged.

Only the bodily resurrection of Christ could have produced this change.

Finally, there is the evidence for the Resurrection which is contemporary and personal. If Jesus Christ rose from the dead, He is alive today, powerful to invade and change those who invite Him into their lives. Thousands now living bear uniform testimony that their lives *have* been revolutionized by Jesus Christ. He has done in them what He said He would do. The proof of the pudding is in the eating. The invitation still stands, "Taste and see that the Lord is good!" The avenue of experimentation is open to each person.

In summary, then, we can agree with Canon Westcott, for years a brilliant scholar at Cambridge, who said, "Indeed, taking all the evidence together, it is not too much to say that there is no historic incident better or more variously supported than the resurrection of Christ. Nothing but the antecedent assumption that it must be false could have suggested the idea of deficiency in the proof of it."[2]

[2]*Westcott, B. F.* The Gospel of the Resurrection, *4th ed., pp. 4-6. London, 1879.*

CHAPTER   5

IS THE BIBLE
GOD'S WORD?

THIS IS A CRUCIAL question and one which is very
much in dispute today. It is, however, not the foremost question in evangelism. Many Christians
think they must prove the Bible to be the Word of
God before they begin to witness. This is not the
case. The crucial issue in salvation is one's relationship to the Lord Jesus Christ—not his view of
the Bible. The Bible *is* the Word of God, regardless
of what a person may think about it, and he can be
led to consider Scripture even before the question
of its inspiration has been settled in his mind.
After conversation with a believer, a person should
realize that the issue is, "What think ye of
Christ?" rather than "What think ye of the
Bible?"

All we need do to confront a person with the
claims of the Lord Jesus Christ is to show him that
the Gospels are reliable historical documents. This
is reasonably easy, as we shall see in a later
chapter. After a person has trusted Christ, the logical question for him to ask is, "How did Christ
view the Bible?" As we shall see, it is abundantly
clear that the Lord Jesus Christ viewed Scripture
as the authoritative Word of God. As a follower of

Christ, the logical step of obedience is to accept His view of the Scripture.

But how can we answer this far-reaching question for ourselves as believers?

While the statements and claims of the Scriptures themselves are not proof, they are a significant body of data which cannot be ignored.

In II Timothy 3:16, we read, "All Scripture is given by inspiration of God and is profitable for doctrine, for reproof, for correction, for instruction in righteousness." The word "inspired," here, is not to be confused with the common usage of the word, as when we say Shakespeare was "inspired" to write great plays or Beethoven was "inspired" to compose great symphonies. Inspiration, in the Biblical sense, is unique. The word translated "inspired" (II Tim. 3:16) actually means "God-breathed." It refers, not to the writers, but to what is written. This is an important point to grasp.

II Peter 1:20, 21 is another important statement "No prophecy of the Scripture is of any private interpretation. For the prophecy came not in old time by the will of man: but holy men of God spake as they were moved by the Holy Ghost." Here again the divine origin of the Scripture is emphasized.

It is important to realize, too, that the writers of the Scripture were not mere writing machines. God did not punch them, like keys on a typewriter, to produce His message. He did not dictate the words, as the Biblical view of inspiration has so often been caricatured. It is quite clear that each writer has a style of his own. Jeremiah does not write like Isaiah, and John does not write like Paul. God worked through the instrumentality of human personality but so guided and controlled men that what they wrote is *what He wanted written*.

Other indications of the claim of supernatural origin of the Scripture are sprinkled throughout its contents. Prophets were consciously God's mouthpieces, and spoke as such: "The word of the Lord came unto me" is a phrase that recurs frequently in the Old Testament. David says, "The spirit of the Lord spoke by me, and His word was in my tongue" (II Sam. 23:2). Jeremiah said, "The Lord put forth His hand and touched my mouth. And the Lord said unto me, 'Behold, I have put My words in thy mouth'" (Jer. 1:9). And Amos cries out, "The Lord God hath spoken, who can but prophesy:" (Amos 3:8)

It is also very remarkable that when later writers of Scripture quote parts of the Scripture which had previously been recorded, they frequently quote it as words spoken by God rather than by a particular prophet. For instance, Paul writes, "And the Scripture, foreseeing that God would justify the heathen through faith, preached before the Gospel unto Abraham saying, 'In thee shall all nations be blessed'" (Gal. 3:8).

There are other passages in which God is spoken of as if He were the Scriptures. For example, "Thou art God . . . who by the mouth of Thy servant, David, hast said, 'Why do the heathen rage and the people imagine a vain thing?'" (Acts 4:24, 25 and Ps. 2:1) Benjamin Warfield points out that these instances of the Scriptures being spoken of as if they were God, and of God being spoken of as if He were the Scriptures, could only result from a habitual identification, in the mind of the writer, of the text of Scripture with God speaking. It became natural, then, to use the term "Scripture said," and to use the term, "God says," when what was really intended was, "Scripture, the Word of God, says. . . ." "The two sets of passages, together, thus show an absolute identification of "Scripture" with the "speaking God."[1]

It is equally clear that New Testament writers have the same prophetic claim to authority as Old Testament writers. Jesus said that John the Baptist was a prophet and more than a prophet (Matt. 11:9-15). As Gordon Clark has put it, "He was superior to all the Old Testament prophets. Yet the prophet who was least in New Testament times was a greater prohet than John. It follows, does it not, that the New Testament prophets were no less inspired than their forerunners?"[2]

Paul claims prophetic authority: "If any man think himself to be a prophet, or spiritual, let him acknowledge that the things that I write unto you are the commandments of the Lord" (I Cor. 14:37).

Peter speaks of Paul's letters as what some "wrest, as they do also the *other* Scriptures, unto their own destruction" (II Peter. 3:16). His reference to them on the same level as "the other Scriptures" shows that he viewed them as having the prophetic authority of Scripture.

Most significant of all, however, is our Lord's view of the Scripture. What did *He* think of it? How did *He* use it. If we can answer this question, we have the answer of the incarnate Word of God Himself. Surely He is the authority for anyone who claims Him as Lord!

What was our Lord's attitude toward the Old Testament? He states emphatically, "Verily I say unto you, Till Heaven and earth pass, one jot or

---

[1] *Warfield, B. B.* The Inspiration and Authority of the Bible, *pp. 299 ff. New York: Oxford University Press, 1927.*

[2] *Clark, Gordon.* Can I Trust My Bible? *pp. 15-16. Chicago: Moody Press, 1963.*

one tittle shall in no wise pass from the Law till all be fulfilled" (Matt. 5:18). He quoted Scripture as final authority, often introducing the statement with the phrase, "It is written," as in His encounter with Satan in the temptation in the wilderness (Matt. 4). He spoke of Himself and of events surrounding His life as being fulfillments of the Scripture (Matt. 26:54, 56).

Perhaps His most sweeping endorsement and acceptance of the Old Testament was when He declared with finality, "The Scripture cannot be broken" (John 10:35).

If, then, we accept Jesus as Saviour and Lord, it would be a contradiction in terms, and strangely inconsistent, if we rejected the Scripture as the Word of God. On this point we would be in disagreement with the One whom we acknowledge to be the eternal God, the Creator of the universe.

Some have suggested that in His view of the Old Testament, our Lord accommodated Himself to the prejudices of His contemporary hearers. They accepted it as authoritative, so He appealed to it to gain wider acceptance for His teaching, though He Himself did not subscribe to the popular view.

Grave difficulties beset this thesis, however. Our Lord's recognition and use of the authority of the Old Testament was not superficial and unessential. It was at the heart of His teaching concerning His person and work. He would be guilty of grave deception, and much of what He taught would be based on a fallacy. Then, too, why would He accommodate Himself at this one point, when on other seemingly less important points He abrasively failed to accommodate Himself to the prejudices of the time? This is most clearly illustrated in His attitude toward the Sabbath. And we could ask an even more basic question: How do we know, if accommodation is His principle of operation, when He is accommodating Himself to ignorance and prejudice and when He is not!

Several definitions will be of great help in our understanding the Bible as the Word of God.

Those who accept the Bible as the Word of God are often accused of taking the Bible "literally." As it is usually put, the question "Do you believe the Bible literally" is like the question, "Have you stopped beating your wife?" Either a Yes or a No convicts the one who responds. Whenever the question is asked, the term "literally" must be carefully defined. Taking a literal view of the Bible does not mean that we do not recognize that figures of speech are used in the Scripture. When Isaiah speaks of the "trees clapping their hands," (Isa. 55:12) and the psalmist of "mountains skipping like rams" (Ps. 114:4.6), it is not to be thought that one who takes the Bible literally views such statements as literal. No, there is poetry as well as prose, and other literary forms, in the Bible. We believe that the Bible is to be interpreted in the sense in which the authors intended it to be received by readers. This is the same principle one employs when reading the newspaper. And it is remarkably easy to distinguish between figures of speech and those statements a writer intends his readers to take literally.

This view is in contrast with that of those who do not take the Bible "literally." They frequently attempt to evade the clear intent of the authority, suggesting that the Biblical records of certain events (for instance, the fall of man, and miracles: are merely nonfactual stories to illustrate and convey profound spiritual truth.

Those holding this view say that as the truth of "Don't kill the goose that lays the golden egg" does not hinge on the literal factuality of Aesop's fable, so we need not insist on the historicity of Biblical events and records to enjoy and realize the truth they convey. Some modern writers have applied this principle even to the cross and the resurrection of Jesus Christ. The expression "Taking the Bible literally," therefore, is ambiguous and must be carefully defined to avoid great confusion.

Another very important term we must clearly define is "inerrancy." What does it mean and what does it not mean? Considerable confusion can be avoided by clear definition at this point.

A temptation we must avoid is that of imposing on the Biblical writers our twentieth century standards of scientific and historical precision and accuracy. For instance, the Scripture describes things phenomenologically—that is as they *appear* to be. It speaks of the sun rising and setting. Now, we know that the sun does not actually rise and set, but that the earth rotates. But we use "sunrise" and "sunset" ourselves, even in an age of scientific enlightenment, because this is a convenient way of describing what appears to be. So we cannot charge the Bible with error when it speaks phenomenologically. Because it speaks in this way, it has been clear to men of all ages and cultures.

In ancient times there were not the same standards of exactness in historical matters. Sometimes round numbers are used rather than precise figures. When the police estimate a crowd we know the figure is not accurate, but it is close enough for the purpose.

Some apparent errors are obviously errors in transcription, which means that careful work is necessary in establishing the true text. We will discuss this more fully in the chapter on whether or not we can trust the Bible documents.

There are some other problems which as yet do not yield a ready explanation. We must freely admit this, remembering that many times, in the past, problems resolved themselves when more data became available. The logical position, then, would seem to be that where there are areas of apparent conflict, we must hold the problem in abeyance, admitting our present inability to explain but awaiting the possibility of new data. The presence of problems does not prevent our accepting the Bible as the supernatural Word of God.

Carnell puts it succinctly: "There is a close parallel between science and Christianity which surprisingly few seem to notice. As Christianity assumes that all in the Bible is supernatural, so the scientist assumes that all in nature is rational and orderly. Both are hypotheses—based, not on all of the evidence, but on the evidence 'for the most part.' Science devoutly holds to the hypothesis that all of nature is mechanical, though as a matter of fact the mysterious electron keeps jumping around as expressed by the Heisenberg principle of uncertainty. And how does science justify its hypothesis that all of nature is mechanical, when it admits on other grounds that many areas of nature do not seem to conform to this pattern? The answer is that since regularity is observed in nature 'for the most part,' the smoothest hypothesis is to assume that it is the same throughout the whole."[3]

A helpful guide to apparent contradictions in the Bible is *Some Alleged Discrepancies in the Bible*, by John W. Haley (Gospel Advocate).

A further indication that the Bible is the Word of God is in the remarkable number of fulfilled pro-

---

[3]*Carnell, E. J.* An Introduction to Christian Apologetics, *p. 208. Grand Rapids: Wm. B. Eerdmans, 1950.*

phecies it contains. These are not vague generalities like those given by modern fortunetellers—"A handsome man will soon come into your life." Such predictions are susceptible to easy misinterpretation. Many Bible prophecies are specific in their details, and the authentication and veracity of the prophet rests on them. The Scripture itself makes it clear that fulfilled prophecy is one of the evidences of the supernatural origin of the word of its prophets (Jer. 28:9). Failure of fulfillment would unmask a false prophet: "If thou say in thine heart, How shall we know the word which the Lord hath not spoken? When a prophet speaketh in the name of the Lord, if the thing follows not, nor comes to pass, that is the thing which the Lord hath not spoken, but the prophet hath spoken it presumptuously: thou shalt not be afraid of him" (Deut. 18:21, 22).

Isaiah ties the unmasking of false prophets to the failure of their predictive prophecy. "Let them bring them forth and show us what shall happen: let them show the former things, what they be, that we may consider them and know the latter end of them: or declare us things for to come. Show the things that are to come hereafter, that we may know that ye are gods" (Isa. 41:22, 23).

There are various kinds of prophecies. One group has to do with predictions of a coming Messiah, the Lord Jesus Christ. Others have to do with specific historical events, and still others with the Jews. It is very significant that the early disciples quoted the Old Testament prophecies frequently to show that Jesus fulfilled in detail the prophecies made many years earlier.

We can mention only a small but representative number of these prophecies. Our Lord refers to the predictive prophecies about Himself in what must have been one of the most exciting Bible studies in history. After conversation with two disciples on the road to Emmaus, He said, "O fools and slow of heart to believe all that the prophets have spoken . . . and beginning at Moses and all the prophets, He expounded unto them in all the Scriptures the things concerning Himself" (Luke 24:25, 27).

Isaiah 52:13—53:12 is the most outstanding example of predictive prophecy about Christ. It is full of contingencies which could not be rigged in advance in an attempt to produce fulfillment. They involve His life, His rejection in ministry, His death, His burial, and His reactions to the unjust judicial proceedings.

Micah 5:2 is a striking illustration of both a prediction about Christ and historic detail. "But thou, Bethlehem Ephratah, though thou be little among the thousands of Judah, yet out of thee shall He come forth unto Me that is to be Ruler in Israel, whose goings forth have been from of old, from everlasting." It took a decree from the mighty Caesar Augustus to bring this event to pass.

Predictions dealt not only with the coming Messiah, but with kings, nations, and cities. Perhaps the most remarkable (Ezek. 26) has to do with the city of Tyre. Here a whole series of little details are given as to how Tyre would be destroyed, the utter completeness of its destruction, and the fact that it would never be reconstructed (cf. v. 4). How this prophecy was fulfilled by degrees, in Nebuchadnezzar's attack and through the savage onslaught of Alexander the Great, is a phenomenal illustration of the accurateness and reality of predictive prophecy in the Bible.

Finally, there are the remarkable prophecies about the Jewish people, the Israelites. Again, only a few of these startling prophecies may be cited.

Their dispersion was predicted by Moses and Hosea. "The Lord shall cause thee to be smitten before thine enemies: thou . . . shalt be removed into all the kingdoms of the earth" (Deut. 28:25). "My God will cast them away, because they did not harken unto Him: and they shall be wanderers among the nations" (Hosea 9:17). Persecution and contempt were predicted: "I will deliver them to be removed into all the kingdoms of the earth for their hurt, to be a reproach and a proverb, a taunt and a curse, in all places whither I shall drive them" (Jer. 24:9). Jeremiah 31 makes the astonishing prediction of the restoration of Israel as a nation. For centuries, this was considered to be unthinkable. Some events in our own time, however, may well be at least partial fulfillment of these prophecies. All observers agree that the reestablishment of Israel as a nation, in 1948, is one of the amazing political phenomena of our day.

One cannot gainsay the force of fulfilled prophecy. Many prophecies could not possibly have been written after the events predicted.

There are, then, a number of pieces of evidence on which one can reasonably base his belief that the Bible *is* the Word of God. As helpful as these evidences are, the testimony of the Holy Spirit is what finally makes one believe that the Bible is the Word of God. As he surveys the evidence and as he reads the Bible, "it dawns on him," to use Gordon Clark's phrase, that the Bible is the Word of God.[4] This realization is the work of the Holy Spirit. But the work of the Spirit is always toward some purpose. This involves the giving of *reasons* for belief, and the explanation of the Scripture message itself.

The two disciples on the road to Emmaus asked,

‘Clark. Op. cit., p. 27.

"Did not our hearts burn within us?" This same experience becomes ours as, by the Holy Spirit, we come to the conviction that the Bible is the Word of God, we feed on it, and we share it with others.

CHAPTER 6

ARE THE BIBLE DOCUMENTS RELIABLE?

SEVERAL YEARS AGO a leading magazine carried an article purporting to show there are thousands of errors in the Bible.

How do we know that the text of the Bible as we have it today, having come to us through many translations and versions over the centuries, is not just a pale reflection of the original? What guarantee do we have that deletions and embellishments have not totally obscured the original message of the Bible? What difference does the historical accuracy of the Bible make? Surely the only thing that counts is the message!

But Christianity is rooted in history. Jesus Christ was counted in a Roman census. If the Bible's historical references are not true, grave questions may be raised about the reliability of other parts of the message based on historical events. Likewise, it is crucial for us to know that we have substantially the same documents in our time as people had almost 2,000 years ago. And how do we know the books we now have are the ones that should be in the Bible? Or that others should not be included? These questions are worthy of answer.

If we believe the Bible to be the Word of God verbally inspired, the job of establishing the text accurately is an extremely important one. This task is called textual criticism. It has to do with the reliability of the text, i.e., how our current text compares with the originals and how accurately the ancient manuscripts were copied.

Let us briefly examine the data for the Old and New Testaments.

It is evident that the work of a scribe was a highly professional and carefully executed task. It was also a task undertaken by a devout Jew with the highest devotion. Since he believed he was dealing with the Word of God, he was acutely aware of the need for extreme care and accuracy. There are no complete copies of the Hebrew Old Testament earlier than around A.D. 900, but it seems evident that the text was preserved very carefully and faithfully since at least A.D. 100 or 200.

A check is provided by comparing some translations from the Hebrew into Latin and Greek at about this time. This comparison reveals the careful copying of the Hebrew text during this period. The text dating from around A.D. 900 is called the "Massoretic Text" because it was the product of Jewish scribes known as the "Massoretes." All of the present copies of the Hebrew text which come from this period are in remarkable agreement, attesting to the skill of the scribes in proofreading.

But how could we know about the accuracy and authenticity of the text in pre-Massoretic times? The history of the Jews was very turbulent, raising questions as to the carefulness of the scribes during this hectic period.

In 1947 the world learned about what has been called the greatest archaeologic discovery of the century. In caves, in the valley of the Dead Sea, ancient jars were discovered containing the now famous Dead Sea Scrolls. From these scrolls, it is evident that a group of Jews lived at a place called Qumran from about 150 B.C. to A.D. 70. Theirs was a communal society, operated very much like a monastery. In addition to tilling the fields, they spent their time studying and copying the Scriptures. It became apparent to them that the Romans were going to invade the land. They put their leather scrolls in jars and hid them in caves in the side of the cliffs west of the Dead Sea.

In the providence of God the scrolls survived undisturbed until discovered accidentally by a wandering Bedouin goat herdsman in February or March of 1947. The accidental discovery was followed by careful exploration, and several other caves containing scrolls have been located. The find included the earliest manuscript copy yet known of the complete book of Isaiah, and fragments of almost every book in the Old Testament. In addition, there is a fragmented copy containing much of Isaiah 38-66. The books of Samuel, in a tattered copy, were also found, along with two complete chapters of Habakkuk. A number of non-biblical items, including the rules of the ancient community, were also discovered.

The significance of this find, for those who wonder about the accuracy of the Old Testament text, can easily be seen. In one dramatic stroke, almost 1,000 years were hurdled in terms of the age of the manuscripts we now possess. By comparing the Dead Sea Scrolls with the Massoretic text, we would get a clear indication of the accuracy, or lack of it, of transmission over the period of nearly a millennium.

What was actually learned? In comparing the

Qumran manuscript of Isaiah 38-66 with the one we had, scholars found that "the text is extremely close to our Massoretic text. A comparison of Isaiah 53 shows that only 17 letters differ from the Massoretic text. Ten of these are mere differences of spelling, like our 'honor' or 'honour,' and produce no change in the meaning at all. Four more are very minor differences, such as the presence of the conjunction, which is often a matter of style. The other three letters are the Hebrew word for 'light' which is added after 'they shall see' in verse 11. Out of 166 words in this chapter, only this one word is really in question, and it does not at all change the sense of the passage. *This is typical of the whole manuscript.*"[1]

Other ancient witnesses attest the accuracy of the copyists who ultimately gave us the Massoretic text. One of these is the Greek translation of the Old Testament, called the Septuagint. It is often referred to as the LXX because it was reputedly done by 70 Jewish scholars in Alexandria. The best estimate of its date seems to be around 200 B.C.

Up till the discovery of the Dead Sea Scrolls there was a question, when the LXX was different from the Massoretic text, why the variation existed. It is now apparent that the Massoretic text has not changed significantly since around 200 B.C. Other scrolls among those discovered show a type of Hebrew that is very similar to that from which the LXX was translated. The Samuel scroll especially resembles the reading of the LXX. The LXX appears to be a rather literal translation, and our

---

[1] *Harris, R. Laird. "How Reliable Is the Old Testament Text? Can I Trust My Bible? p. 124. Chicago: Moody Press, 1963. Consult this work for a fuller but brief discussion of this question.*

manuscripts are pretty good copies of the original translation.

Another ancient witness is the evidence for a third type of text similar to that which was preserved by the Samaritans. Copies of the old scrolls of the Pentateuch are extant today in Nablus, Palestine.

Three main types of text existed in 200 B.C. The question for us is, What is the *original* version of the Old Testament, in the light of these three "families" of texts to choose from?

We can conclude with R. Laird Harris, "We can now be sure that copyists worked with great care and accuracy on the Old Testament, even back to 225 B.C. At that time there were two or three types of text available for copying. These types differed among themselves so little, however, that we can infer that still earlier copyists had also faithfully and carefully transmitted the Old Testament text. Indeed, it would be rash skepticism that would now deny that we have our Old Testament in a form very close to that used by Ezra when he taught the Law to those who had returned from the Babylonian captivity."[2]

What of the New Testament? Again, based on the evidence, the conviction comes that we have in our hands a text which does not differ in any substantial particular from the originals of the various books as they came from the hands of the human writers. The great scholar, F. J. A. Hort, said that apart from insignificant variations of grammar or spelling, not more than one thousandth part of the whole New Testament is affected by differences of reading.[3]

---

[2]Ibid., *pp. 129, 130*.
[3]*Westcott, B. F., and Hort, F. J. A., eds.* New Testament in Original Greek, *Vol. II, p. 2, 1881.*

The New Testament was written in Greek. More than 4,000 manuscripts of the New Testament, or of parts of it, have survived to our time. These are on different materials. Papyrus was the common material use for writing purposes at the beginning of the Christian era. It was made from reeds and was highly durable. In the last 500 years many remains of documents written on papyrus have been discovered, including fragments of manuscripts of the New Testament.

The second material of which Greek manuscripts were made is parchment. This was the skin of sheep or goats, polished with pumice. It was used until the late Middle Ages, when paper began to replace it.

The dates of the New Testament documents indicate that they were written within the lifetime of contemporaries of Christ. People were still alive who could remember the things He said and did. Many of the Pauline letters are even earlier than some of the Gospels.[4]

The evidence for the early existence of the New Testament writings is clear. The wealth of materials for the New Testament becomes even more evident when we compare it with other ancient documents which have been accepted without question. Bruce observes that only nine or ten good manuscripts of Caesar's *Gallic War* exist. The oldest of these manuscripts was written some 900 years after Caesar's time. The *History of Thucydides* (ca. 460-400 B.C.) is known to us from eight manuscripts, the earliest belonging to around A.D. 900, and a few papyrus scraps that belong to about the

---

[4]*Bruce, F. F.* The New Testament Documents: Are They Reliable? *Grand Rapids: Wm. B. Eerdmans. Contains a full discussion of the dating of documents and other related questions.*

beginning of the Christian era. The same is true of the *History of Herodotus* (ca. 480-425 B.C.). However, no classical scholar would listen to an argument that the authenticity of Herodotus or Thucydides is in doubt because of the earliest manuscripts of their work which are of any use to us are more than 1,300 years later than the originals."[5]

By contrast there are two excellent manuscripts of the New Testament from the fourth century. Fragments of papyrus copies of books of the New Testament date from 100 to 200 years earlier still. Perhaps the earliest piece of data we have is a fragment of a papyrus codex containing John 18:31-33, 37. It is dated around A.D. 130.

More evidence for the authenticity of the New Testament comes from other sources. These are the references and quotations of the New Testament books by both friends and enemies of Christianity. The Apostolic Fathers, writing mostly between A.D. 90 and 160, give indication of familiarity with most of the books of the New Testament.

It seems apparent, from recent discoveries, that the Gnostic school of Valentinus was also familiar with most of the New Testament.[6]

There are two other sources of data for establishing the authenticity of the New Testament books. The first source is the versions. Versions are those manuscripts which were translated from the Greek into other languages. Three groups of these are of the most significance: the Syriac versions, the Egyptian or Coptic versions, and the Latin versions. By careful study of the versions, important clues have been uncovered as to the original Greek manuscripts from which they were translated.

[5] Ibid., *pp. 16, 17.*

[6] Ibid., *p. 19.*

Finally, there is the evidence of the lectionaries, the reading lessons used in public church services. By the middle of the twentieth century more than 1,800 of these reading lessons had been classified. There are lectionaries of the Gospels, The Acts, and the Epistles. Though they did not appear before the sixth century, the text from which they quote may itself be early and of high quality.[7]

Though there have been many changes in the many copyings of the New Testament writings, most of them are minor. The science of textual criticism, which is very exacting, has enabled us to be sure of the true text of the New Testament. Rather than share the "alarm" of *Look* magazine at all the "errors" which it chose to call those minor variations in the Bible, we can rest with the conclusion of the late Sir Frederic Kenyon, a world-renowned scholar of the ancient manuscripts. He said, "The interval, then, between the dates of original composition and the earliest extant evidence becomes so small as to be in fact negligible, and the last foundation for any doubt that the Scriptures have come down to us substantially as they were written has now been removed. Both the authenticity and the general integrity of the books of the New Testament may be regarded as finally established."[8]

A question closely allied to that of the reliability of the texts we have is, "How do we know the books in our Bible, and no others, are the ones that should be there?" This is called the question of the

---

[7]*Mickelsen, A. Berkley. "Is the Text of the New Testament Reliable? Can I Trust My Bible? p. 160.*

[8]*Kenyon, Sir Frederic. The Bible and Archaeology (pp. 288 ff.) 1940, as quoted by F. F. Bruce in The New Testament Document: Are They Reliable? (p. 20). Grand Rapids: Wm. B. Eerdmans.*

canon. There are distinct questions involved for Old and New Testaments.

The Protestant Church accepts identically the same Old Testament books as the Jews had, and as Jesus and the apostles accepted. The Roman Catholic Church, since the Council of Trent in 1546, includes the 14 books of the Apocrypha. The order in the English Bible follows that of the Septuagint. This is different from the Hebrew Bible, in which the books are divided into three groups: the Law (Genesis to Deuteronomy), known also as the Torah or the Pentateuch; the Prophets, including the Former Prophets (Joshua, Judges, Samuel, Kings) and the Latter Prophets (Isaiah, Jeremiah, Ezekiel, and the Book of the Twelve—Hosea to Malachi), and the Writings, the remaining books of our Old Testament canon.

The books were received as authoritative because they were recognized as utterances of men inspired by God to reveal His Word. As E. J. Young says, "When the Word of God was written, it became Scripture, and inasmuch as it had been spoken by God, it possessed absolute authority. Since it was the Word of God, it was canonical. That which determines the canonicity of a book, therefore, is the fact that the book is inspired of God. Hence, a distinction is properly made between the authority which the Old Testament books possess as divinely inspired and the recognition of that authority on the part of Israel."[9]

We can see this development in the work of Moses. The laws issued by him and by the later prophets were intended to be respected as the de-

---

[9]*Young, E. J. "The Canon of the Old Testament,"* Revelation and the Bible, *p. 156; ed. C. F. Henry. Grand Rapids: Baker Book House, 1956.*

crees of God Himself. They were so regarded then and also by later generations. The Law was neglected, to be sure, but its authority was recognized by Israel's spiritual leaders. It was the recognition of this authority that shook Josiah when he realized how long the Law had been neglected (II Kings 22:11).

When we examine the writings of the prophets, it is obvious that they believed they spoke with authority. "Thus saith the Lord" and "The Word of the Lord came unto me saying" are common preambles to their messages.

It is not clear on what grounds the authority of the writings was accepted. That it *was* accepted, however, *is* clear. In New Testament times it was customary to describe at least some of these writings as the utterances of the Holy Spirit.

By the beginning of the Christian era the term "Scripture" had come to mean a fixed body of divinely inspired writings that were fully recognized as authoritative. Our Lord used the term in this sense and was fully understood by His hearers when He said, "The Scripture cannot be broken" (John 10:35). It is interesting that there was no controversy between our Lord and the Pharisees on the authority of the Old Testament. Contention arose because they had added their *tradition* and had given it the same authority as Scripture.

At the Council of Jamnia, in A.D. 90, informal discussions were held about the canon. Whether any formal or binding decisions were made is problematic. The discussion seemed to center not on whether certain books should be included in the canon, but whether certain ones should be excluded. In any case, those present recognized what already was accepted, rather than brought into being what had not existed. In other words, they *recog-*

73

nized but did not *establish* the canonicity of the Old Testament books as we have them.

The Apocryphal books, it is important to note, were never received into the Jewish canon and were not considered as part of the inspired Scriptures by Jews or Christians in the early centuries of the Christian era. This is evident from a study of the writings of Josephus, the Jewish historian, and of Augustine, the great North African Bishop of Hippo.

It is interesting that the New Testament writers do not once quote the Apocrypha.

The Apocryphal books do not claim to be the Word of God or the work of prophets. They vary greatly in content and value. Some, like I Maccabees, were probably written around 100 B.C. and are valuable as historical background. Others are more characterized by legend and are of little value. Thought not included at first, these books were later added to the LXX. In this way they came to be included by Jerome in the Latin Vulgate. Even Jerome, however, accepted only the books in the Hebrew Canon. He viewed the others as having ecclesiastical value only. He was in conflict with the later action of the Council of Trent, in Reformation times, which elevated the Apocrypha to canonical status.

For the Old Testament we have, ultimately, the witness of our Lord to the canonicity of the 39 books we now have.

What about the books of the New Testament?

Here, as for the Old Testament, the books possessed canonicity by virtue of their inspiration, not by virtue of their being "voted" into canonicity by any group. The history of the recognition of the New Testament's canonicity, however, is interesting. Much of the material of the New Testament claimed apostolic authority. Paul and Peter clearly wrote with this authority in mind. Peter specifically refers to Paul's letters as Scripture (II Pet. 3:15, 16).

Jude (v. 18) says II Peter 3:3 is a word from the apostles. Such early Church Fathers as Polycarp, Ignatius, and Clement mention a number of the New Testament books as authoritative.

The onslaught of heresy in the middle of the second century caused the concept of a canon to be revived in the thinking of Christians. What was authoritative and what was not came to be clearly delineated. Irenaeus, and later Eusebius in the third century, give us more light in their writings. The final fixation of the canon as we know it came in the fourth century. In the east, a letter of Athanasius in A.D. 367 clearly distinguishes between works in the canon which are described as the sole sources of religious instruction and others which believers were permitted to read. In the west, the canon was fixed by decision of a church council held at Carthage in A.D. 397.

Three criteria were generally utilized, throughout this period of time, to establish that particular written documents were the true record of the voice and message of apostolic witness. First, could authorship be attributed to an apostle? The Gospels of Mark and Luke do not meet this criterion specifically, but were accepted as the works of close associates of the apostles. Secondly, there was the matter of ecclesiastical usage—that is, recognition of a book by a leading church or majority of churches. Third, conformity to standards of sound doctrine.

These data are helpful and interesting, but in the final analysis, as with the question of the inspiration of the Scripture, canonicity is a question of the witness of the Spirit in the hearts of God's people.

In days of uncertainty, what a rock the Scripture is on which to stand! "Heaven and earth shall pass away," says our Lord, "but My Word shall never pass away!"

CHAPTER 7

DOES ARCHAEOLOGY HELP?

ONE OF THE STRANGE paradoxes of our time is the extent to which more and more people are questioning the reliability of the Scripture, in spite of the fact that there is greater evidence than ever for its trustworthiness. More than a century ago critics questioned many historical statements in the Old Testament. They thought them fictional and highly imaginative. But our century is one of unprecedented discovery, and these discoveries have for the most part substantiated the Biblical record. The statements of nonevangelical scholars are significant. Dr. W. F. Albright, professor emeritus of Johns Hopkins University says, "There can be no doubt that archaeology has confirmed the substantial historicity of Old Testament tradition."[1]

Millar Burrows, of Yale, states, "On the whole, however, archaeological work has unquestionably strengthened confidence in the reliability of the Scriptural record. More than one archaeologist has found his respect for the Bible increased by the ex-

---

[1]*Vos, Howard F.* An Introduction to Bible Archaeology, *p. 121, quoting from W. F. Albright's* Archaeology and the Religion of Israel. *Chicago: Moody Press, n.d.*

perience of excavation in Palestine."[2] He also says, "Archaeology has in many cases refuted the views of modern critics. It has shown, in a number of instances, that these views rest on false assumptions and unreal, artificial schemes of historical development. This is a real contribution and not to be minimized."[3]

Sir Frederic Kenyon, a former director of the British Museum, writes, "It is therefore legitimate to say that, in respect of that part of the Old Testament against which the disintegrating criticism of the last half of the nineteenth century was chiefly directed, the evidence of archaeology has been to reestablish its authority and likewise to augment its value by rendering it more intelligible through fuller knowledge of its background and setting. Archaeology has not yet said its last word, but the results already achieved confirm what faith would suggest—that the Bible can do nothing but gain from an increase in knowledge."[4]

More recently, Nelson Glueck, renowned Jewish archaeologist, made the remarkable statement, "No archaeological discovery has ever controverted a Biblical reference."[5]

Clearly then, archaeology is of great value in giving us a clearer understanding of the Biblical record and message by enabling us to understand the background into which it is set. It is also clear that certain points of apparent conflict between the Biblical record and the information previously available have been cleared up as more information

[2]*Burrows, Millar*. What Mean These Stones? *p. 1.* New Haven: American Schools of Oriental Research, 1941, *as quoted by H. F. Vos in* op. cit.

[3]Ibid., *pp. 291, 292.*

[4]*Kenyon, Sir Frederic.* Op. cit., *p. 279.*

[5]*Glueck, Nelson.* Rivers in the Desert, *p. 31.*

has been obtained. It would seem, then, that the logical attitude toward a still existing area of apparent conflict would be to hold the matter in abeyance. Rather than conclude that the Bible must be wrong, it would seem much more reasonable to admit the problem exists and to hold it open pending further discoveries. Since new discoveries, time after time in the past, have tended to confirm the Scripture, this would certainly be a more reasonable attitude than declaring the Bible wrong out of hand.

Having said all this, however, it is important to point out that we cannot "prove" the Bible by archaeology, nor do we *believe* the Bible on the basis of archaeological "proof." It is the Holy Spirit who ultimately confirms the truth of the Scripture to us. Spiritual truth can never be confirmed by archaeology. But we can be thankful for the historical details which have been confirmed by archaeology even though we recognize the apparent conflicts that still exist.

What are some of the specific ways in which archaeology has been of help?

More than 25,000 sites showing some connection with the Old Testament period have been located in Bible lands. Relatively few have been explored, so a wealth of material awaits discovery.

The largest body of evidence for comparison with Scriptures is found in the ancient Eastern inscriptions. Very few contemporary documents from Old Testament times have been found in Palestine itself. Illustrations must be drawn from the writings of neighboring countries.

Another major source of information for comparison with Biblical narratives has been the archaeological excavation of Biblical sites.

The field of information and correlation with

Biblical data is vast, so we can spotlight only a few of the major facets.

The life and times of Abraham are a good example of the help archaeology can be to us. Critics of the latter part of the last century and the early years of this one were very dubious about the historicity of the Biblical account of Abraham. They thought he was an ignorant nomad and quite primitive. They felt he would be unable to read and would have no more knowledge of law, history, commerce, and geography than a Bedouin sheikh in the Arabian desert today. They believed that for him to move from Ur to Haran was merely a minor nomadic shift. But the discoveries of Sir C. Leonard Woolley in his excavations at Ur of the Chaldees have shown these ideas to have been serious mistakes.

We have discovered that the Ur of Abraham's time was a highly developed city. Archaeologists have unearthed advanced housing and many clay tablets which were the equivalent of books. Some of these were receipts for business transactions; others were temple hymns; others were mathematical tables with formulae for calculating square and cube roots as well as simpler sums. In the temple storerooms, receipts were found for numberless objects—sheep, cheese, wool, cooper ore, oil for lubrication of hinges—and payrolls for female employees. It is all very practical and curiously modern.[6]

It "became clear that Abraham was a product of a brilliant and highly developed culture, and that it must have meant a good deal for him to leave by faith for unknown lands."[7]

---

[6]*Short, A. Rendle.* Op. cit., *p. 137.*

[7]*Vos, Howard F.* Genesis and Archaeology, *p. 52. Chicago: Moody Press, 1963.*

How can these finds be dated? "These ancient cities were built and rebuilt on the same site, so that a whole succession of levels is usually found, the lowest naturally being the oldest. Fashions in pottery changed, and if at one excavated site a particular fashion can be dated, similar pottery found elsewhere will be of the same period. Kings usually inscribed their names on the hinge-sockets of temple doors, and the name of the god would be given. Inscribed stones were often laid under palace or temple walls in memory of the founder. Royal sepulchres can usually be identified in the same way. There exist copies, dating back before 2000 B.C., of lists drawn up by Sumerian scribes of the kings according to the successive dynasties with notes as to the lengths of their reigns. A few miles from Ur an inscribed foundation-stone was found, laid by a king of known name, of the First Dynasty of Ur, which the scribes speak of as the third dynasty after the Flood. This king seems to have reigned 3,100 years before Christ, more than a thousand years before Abraham.[8]

Archaeology provides considerable background information for the study of the Biblical kings. Critics have questioned the historicity of these accounts. The accounts of Solomon's grandeur have met special skepticism. The Bible speaks of him as having a navy (I Kings 9:26), though there is no suitable harbor on the coastline of Palestine. It describes his wealth as being staggering, the number of his horses and chariots as astounding (10:26). His building projects were numerous and extensive. He fortified the cities of Jerusalem, Hazor, Gezer, and Megiddo (9:15). Extensive excavation has been undertaken at Megiddo. Interesting details of

---

[8]*Short.* Op. cit., *p. 138.*

this military installation have come to light. Of particular interest are Solomon's stables.

"A wide paved street led from the city gate of Megiddo to the stables of Solomon. The southern stable compound measured about 70 by 92 yards. A row of five stable units faced north and opened onto a courtyard or parade ground approximately 60 yards on a side. A wall, more than a yard thick in some places, was then built around the grounds to prevent the sand from washing away. Near the center of the courtyard was a sunken cistern of mud-dried bricks which was probably used as a water tank for the horses; this was capable of holding some 2,775 gallons of water. Two rectangular rooms along one side of the enclosure probably served as chariot garages.

"Each stable unit consisted of a central passage about ten feet wide, floored with lime plaster. On either side of this was an aisle of similar width, separated from the central passageway by a row of stone pillars alternating with stone mangers which had troughs measuring about five feet in width and paved with rubble. Each aisle was 26 yards in length and cared for 15 horses, making a total of 150 for the southern compound."[9]

Solomon's casting of metals is mentioned in II Kings. In the excavation of Ezion-Geber one of the most spectacular finds was the blast furnace. Nelson Glueck says, "The finest and largest smelting and refining plant ever discovered in the ancient Near East has been unearthed at the northwest corner of the site. It was provided with a compli-

[9]*Vos, Howard F.* An Introduction to Bible Archaeology, *p. 75. Chicago: Moody Press, 1956.*

[10]*Glueck, Nelson. "Ezion-Geber,"* Bulletin of the American Schools of Oriental Research, *Oct., 1939, p. 10, as quoted by Vos, ibid.*

cated system of flues and air channels almost modern in aspect and function."[10] The fierce winds which blew through the Arabah to the north were harnessed to eliminate the necessity of artificial bellows. To this refinery in Solomon's seaport was brought ore which had been partially processed in ovens along the length of the Southern Arabah (the valley extending from the south end of the Dead Sea to the Red Sea). Most of the present knowledge of these Arabah mining sites depends also upon the work of Nelson Glueck. For instance, he excavated Khirget Hahas (Arabic for "copper ruin") about 21 miles south of the Dead Sea. Ores were surface-mined near here and put through the initial roasting process.

"The site is oblong, pointed north and south. A semicircular range of high sandstone hills surrounds it. On the east is a small wadi (a stream that does not flow during the dry season). Between the hills on the south and west, with the wadi on the east and north sides, lies a large flat area packed with ruins of walls, large buildings, miners' huts, smelting furnaces, and huge heaps of black copper slag. Two furnaces, a square and a circular one, are almost intact. The square one is of roughly hewn blocks three yards square and contains two compartments, one above the other."[11]

A remarkable memorial, commemorating one of the few incidents in the history of Moab of which we have any record, has survived. After Ahab died, Mesha, the king of Moab, threw off the yoke of Jehoram, Ahab's son, and refused to pay tribute. He was put under siege by the kings of Israel, Judah, and Edom. So great was the pressure that Mesha finally offered his eldest son on the wall as a burnt

[11]*Vos.* Ibid., *pp. 79, 80.*

offering to Chemosh, the god of the Moabites. What happened then is not clear, but the implication is that the three kings had to abandon their siege.

In 1868 a German named Klein found an inscribed stone at Dibon, in the land of Moab. While he was back in Europe to raise money for its purchase, the Arabs roasted the stone and threw cold water over it to break it into pieces and so get a larger price. Fortunately, an impression had been taken of the intact stone, so it was possible to restore the fragments and read the inscription. The stone is now at the Louvre in Paris. The inscription is an early form of the Phoenician alphabet and describes how the stone was set up by Mesha, King of Moab, to tell how he, with the help of Chemosh his god, had thrown off the yoke of the King of Israel. A number of Biblical place-names are mentioned and the God of Israel is called Yahweh.[12]

Archaeological research and discovery for the New Testament has been of a different nature than for the Old. It is not so much a matter of digging for buried buildings or inscribed tablets; rather, New Testament archaeology is primarily a matter of written documents.

"These documents may be public or private inscriptions on stone or some equally durable material; they may be papyri recovered from the sand of Egypt recording literary texts or housewives' shopping lists; they may be private notes scratched on fragments of unglazed pottery; they may be legends on coins preserving information about some otherwise forgotten ruler or getting some point of official propaganda across to the people who used them. They may represent a Christian church's

[12]*Short,* Op. cit., *p. 184.*

collection of sacred Scriptures, like the Chester Beatty Biblical Papyri; they may be all that is left of the library of an ancient religious community, like the scrolls from Qumran or the Gnostic texts from Nag Hammadi. But whatever their character, they can be as important and relevant for the study of the New Testament as any cuneiform tablets are for the study of the Old."[13]

Papyrus documents have yielded a wealth of information. The common people wrote letters on papyrus and kept the ordinary commercial accounts of life on it. An even cheaper writing material was broken pieces of pottery, called *ostraca*. These were used for odd notes. One of the great significances of these materials, discovered in ancient rubbish heaps, has been to show the connection between the everyday language of the common people and the Greek in which most of the New Testament is written. It has long been recognized that there are great differences between the Greek of classic literature and that of the New Testament. Some scholars went so far as to suggest that New Testament Greek was a heavenly language which came into being for the purpose of recording Christian revelation. But through the discoveries of the papyri it became evident that the New Testament Greek was very similar to the language of the common people.

In 1931 the discovery of a collection of papyrus texts of the Greek Scriptures was made public. They have come to be known as the "Chester Beatty Biblical Papyri." F. F. Bruce says that this collection evidently formed the Bible of some outlying church in Egypt; it comprises 11 fragmentary

---

[13]*Bruce, F. F. "Archaeological Confirmation of the New Testament,"* Revelation and the Bible, *p. 320; ed. by C. F. Henry. Grand Rapids: Baker Book House, 1958.*

codices. Three of these, in their complete state, contained most of the New Testament. One contained the Gospels and Acts, another Paul's nine letters to churches and the Epistle to the Hebrews, and a third the Revelation. All three were written in the third century. The Pauline codex, oldest of the three, was written at the beginning of that century. Even in their present mutilated state, these papyri bear most important testimony to the early textual history of the New Testament. They have provided most valuable evidence for the identification of the "Caesarean" text-type.[14]

These examples show the importance of papyrus discoveries.

Inscriptions on stone have been another source of valuable information. An example of this is an edict of Claudius inscribed on limestone at Delphi in Central Greece. "This edict is to be dated [as originating] during the first seven months of A.D. 52, and mentions Gallio as being proconsul of Achaia. We know from other sources that Gallio's proconsulship lasted only for a year, and since proconsuls entered on their term of office on July 1, the inference is that Gallio entered on his proconsulship on that date in A.D. 51. But Gallio's proconsulship of Achaia overlapped Paul's year and a half of ministry in Corinth (Acts 18:11, 12) so that Claudius' inscription provides us with a fixed point for reconstructing the chronology of Paul's career."[15]

Luke makes so many specific references to people and places that his writings are more easily illustrated by this kind of material than other parts of the New Testament. His accuracy of detail has been thoroughly established. Where he has been

[14]Ibid., p. 323.
[15]Ibid., p. 324.

questioned, new evidence has vindicated him a number of times. Bruce points out, "For example, his reference in Luke 3:1 to 'Lysanias, the tetrarch of Abilene,' at the time when John the Baptist began his ministry A.D. 27 has been regarded as a mistake because the only ruler of that name in those parts known from ancient historians was King Lysanias, whom Antony executed at Cleopatra's instigation in 36 B.C. But a Greek inscription from Abila (18 miles west-northwest of Damascus), from which the territory of Abilene is named, records a dedication to one Nymphaeus, 'freeman of Lysanias, the tetrarch' between A.D. 14-29, around the very time indicated by Luke."[16]

An unusual bit of data was discovered in 1945. Eleazar L. Sukenik found two ossuaries, or receptacles for bones, in the vicinity of the Jerusalem suburb of Talpioth. The burial chamber in which these were found was in use during the years preceding A.D. 50. It is possible, says Bruce, "that here we have relics from the Christian community in Jerusalem during the first 20 years of its existence."[17]

Coins have provided some background information for parts of New Testament history. One of the crucial questions in establishing the chronology of Paul's career is the date of Felix's replacement by Festus as procurator of Judea (Acts 24:27). A new Judean coinage begins in Nero's fifth year, before October of A.D. 59. This may point to the beginning of the new procuratorship.

Some sacred sites have been definitely identified, and general locations have also been identified. General locations have been more easily estab-

---

[16]Ibid., p. 327.
[17]Ibid., p. 328.

lished than exact spots where some of the great New Testament events transpired. Jerusalem was destroyed in A.D. 70 and a new pagan city was founded on the site in A.D. 135. This has complicated the identification of places in Jerusalem mentioned in the Gospels and Acts. Some, however, like the Temple area and the pool of Siloam, to which our Lord sent the blind man to wash (John 9:11), have been clearly identified.

Archaeology is a real help in understanding the Bible. It yields fascinating information which illuminates what might otherwise be obscured, and in some instances confirms what some might otherwise regard as doubtful.

We can agree with Sir Frederic Kenyon when he says, "To my mind, the true and valuable thing to say about archaeology is, not that it proves the Bible, but that it illustrates the Bible. . . . The contribution of archaeology to Bible study has been to ground of the Bible narrative, and especially of the Old Testament. . . . The trend of all this increased knowledge has been to confirm the authority of the books of the Old Testament while it illuminates their interpretation. Destructive criticism is thrown on the defensive; and the plain man may read his Bible confident that, for anything that modern research has to say, the Word of our God shall stand forever."[18]

[18]*Sir Frederic Kenyon, as quoted by A. Rendle Short in* Modern Discovery and the Bible.

CHAPTER 8

ARE MIRACLES POSSIBLE?

"Do you really believe Jonah was swallowed by a whale? And do you seriously think that Christ *actually* fed 5,000 persons from five loaves of bread and two fish?" So goes the trend and tone of many modern questioners. Surely, they say, these "miracle" stories in the Bible must be quaint ways of conveying spiritual truth, and they are not meant to be taken literally.

With many questions, it is more important to discern the root problem than to become involved in discussing a twig on a branch. This is especially true of questions about miracles. The questioner's problem is generally not with a particular miracle, but with a whole principle. To establish the miracle in question would not answer his question. His controversy is with the whole principle of the possibility of miracles.

One who has problems with miracles often also has difficulty with the validity of predictive prophecy. These problems stem from a weak view of God. The real problem, then, is not with miracles or prophecy but with the whole concept of God.

Once we assume the existence of God, there is no problem with miracles, because God is by definition all-powerful. In the absence of such a God, however, the concept of miracles is extremely difficult, if not impossible, to entertain.

This came to me very forcibly one day as I was talking about the deity of Christ with a Japanese professor friend. "I find it very difficult to believe," he said, "that a man could become God." Sensing his problem, I replied, "Yes, Kinichi, so do I, but I can believe that God became a man." He saw the difference in a flash, and not long afterward he became a Christian.

The question, then, really is, "Does an all-powerful God, who created the universe, exist?" If so, we shall have little difficulty with miracles in which He transcends the natural law of which He is the Author. It is important to keep this fundamental question in mind in discussing miracles.

Why we know God exists has already been discussed.

David Hume and others have defined a miracle as a violation of natural law. To take such a position, however, is practically to deify natural law, to capitalize it in such a way that whatever God there may be becomes the prisoner of natural law and, in effect, ceases to be God.

In this modern scientific age, men tend to personify science and natural law. They fail to realize that these are merely the impersonal results of observation. A Christian believes in natural law—i.e., that things behave in a certain cause-and-effect way almost all the time. But in maintaining this he does not restrict God's right and power to intervene when and how He chooses. God is over, above, and outside natural law, and is not bound by it.

Laws do not *cause* anything in the sense that

God causes things. They are merely descriptions of what happens.

What, in fact, is a miracle? We use the term rather loosely today. If a scared student passes an exam he says, "It was a miracle!" Or if an old jalopy makes a successful trip from one city to another, we say, "It's a miracle the thing ran!" We use the term to mean anything that is unusual or unexpected. We do not necessarily mean that the hand of God has been at work.

In discussing miracles as they are thought of in the Bible, however, the word is used in an entirely different sense. Here we mean an act of God breaking into, changing, or interrupting the ordinary course of things.

To be sure, the Bible records various kinds of miracles, and some of them *could* have a "natural" explanation. For instance, the parting of the Red Sea was accomplished by the "natural" cause of the high winds which drove the waters back. Perhaps this *could* have happened apart from God's intervention. The miraculous part was the timing. That the waters should part just as the Israelites reached the shore, and should close on the Egyptians as they were in hot pursuit and after every Israelite was safely on dry land, clearly proves the miraculous intervention of God.

On the other hand, there are many miracles for which there are no "natural" explanations. The resurrection of Lazarus from the dead and the resurrection of our Lord involved forces unknown to us and outside the realm of so-called natural law. The same is true with many of the miraculous healings. It has been fashionable to explain these in terms of psychosomatic response. We know today that many illnesses, rather than having an organic origin, originate in the mind. If the mental condition is corrected, the physical condition rights itself. Some medical authorities estimate that upwards of 80 percent of the illnesses in our pressurized society are psychosomatic.

Undoubtedly there was an element of this dimension in our Lord's healings, but some were clearly outside this category. Take, for instance, the healings of leprosy. Obviously these did not have a psychosomatic base. Lepers who were made well experienced the direct power of God. Then there are the clear cases of healing of congenital disease, such as the man born blind (John 9). Since this man was born with his blindness, it could obviously not be accounted for on a psychosomatic basis, and for the same reasons neither could his receiving his sight.

This case illustrates the fallacy of another notion common among modern thinkers. We must remember, it is said, that people in ancient times were exceedingly ignorant, gullible, and superstitious. They thought many things were miracles that we now know, with the benefit of modern science, were not miracles at all but simply phenomena which people didn't understand. For instance, if we were to fly a modern jet over a primitive tribe today, they would probably fall to the ground in worship of this Silver Bird God of the sky. They would think that the sight they observed was a miraculous phenomenon. We, however, know that the plane is simply a result of the applied principles of aerodynamics, and we realize there is nothing miraculous about it at all.

The problem with this thesis, which sounds so plausible at first, is that many of the miracles are not of this order. In the case of the blind man, the people observed that since the beginning of time it had not been known for a man born blind to receive his sight. And we have no more "natural" explanation of this miracle now than was available then. And who, today, has any more explanation, in a natural sense, of our Lord's resurrection from the dead than was available when it happened? No one! We simply cannot get away from the supernatural aspects of the Biblical record.

It is important to note, however, that miracles are not in conflict with natural law. Rather, "Miracles are *unusual* events caused by God. The laws of nature are generalizations about ordinary events caused by Him."[1]

There are two views among thinking Christians as to the relationship of miracles to natural law. Some suggest that miracles employ a "higher" natural law, which at present is unknown to us. It is quite obvious that despite all of the impressive discoveries of modern science, we are still standing on the seashore of an ocean of ignorance. When we have increased our knowledge sufficiently, this thesis says, we will realize that the things we today thought were miracles were merely the working out of higher laws of the universe, of which we were not aware at the time.

But a "law," in the modern scientific sense, is that which is regular and acts uniformly. To say that a miracle is the result of a higher "law," then, is to use the term in a way that is different from its customary usage and meaning.

On the other hand, there are those Christian thinkers who view miracles as an act of creation—a sovereign, transcendent act of God's supernatural power. It would seem that this is the more appropriate view.

---

[1] *Hawthorne, J. N.* Questions of Science and Faith, *p. 55. London: Tyndale Press, 1960.*

Biblical miracles, in contrast to miracle stories in pagan literature and those of other religions, were never capricious or fantastic. They are not scattered helter-skelter through the record without rhyme or reason. There was always clear order and purpose to them. They cluster around three periods of Biblical history; the Exodus, the prophets who led Israel, and the time of Christ and the early Church. They always had as their purpose to confirm faith by authenticating the message and the messenger, or to demonstrate God's love by relieving suffering. They were never performed as entertainment, as a magician puts on a show for his patrons.

Miracles were never performed for personal prestige or to gain money or power. Our Lord was tempted by the Devil in the wilderness to use His miracle power in just this way, but He steadfastly refused. As an evidence of the truth of the Christian message, however, our Lord referred to miracles frequently. In answer to the direct request of the Jews to tell them plainly if He was the Messiah, He said, "I told you and ye believed not: the works that I do in My Father's name, they bear witness of Me" (John 10:25). Again He says that if they had any hesitation in believing His claims they should believe Him "for the very works' sake" (14:11).

God confirmed the message of the apostles in the fledgling Church with signs and wonders.

The question is often raised, "If God performed miracles *then*, why does He not do them *now*? If I *saw* a miracle I could believe!" This question was answered in our Lord's time. A rich man who was in the torment of hell lifted up his eyes and pleaded with Abraham that someone should warn his five brothers lest they too should come into the awful place. He was told that his brothers had the Scriptures. But the rich man protested that if one should rise from the dead, they would be shaken by the miracle and would take heed. The reply given applies as much today as then: "They have Moses and the prophets," Abraham said, "and if they hear not Moses and the prophets, neither will they be persuaded though one rose from the dead" (Luke 16). And so it is today. Many have made a rationalistic presupposition which rules out the very possibility of miracles. Since they *know* miracles are impossible, no amount of evidence would ever persuade them one had taken place. There would always be an alternate naturalistic explanation for them to advance.

Miracles are not necessary for us today because we already have reliable records of those miracles which have occurred. As Ramm observes, "If miracles are capable of sensory perception, they can be made matters of testimony. If they are adequately testified to, then the recorded testimony has the same validity for evidence as the experience of beholding the event."[2]

Every court in the world operates on the basis of reliable testimony by word of mouth or in writing. "If the raising of Lazarus was actually witnessed by John and recorded faithfully by him when still in soundness of faculties and memory, for purposes of evidence it is the same as if we were there and saw it."[3] Ramm then lists reasons we may know that the miracles have adequate and reliable testimony. We summarize:

First, many miracles were done in public. They were not performed in secret before only one or

---

[2]*Ramm.* Op. cit., *p. 140.*
[3]Ibid., *pp. 140, 141.*

two people, who announced them to the world. There was every opportunity to investigate the miracles on the spot. It is very impressive that the opponents of Jesus never denied the fact of the miracles He performed. They either attributed them to the power of Satan or else tried to suppress the evidence, as with the raising of Lazarus from the dead. They said, "Let's kill Him before the people realize what is happening and the whole world goes after Him!"

Second, some miracles were performed before unbelievers. It is significant that the miracles claimed by cults and offbeat groups never seem to happen when the skeptic is present to observe. It was not so with Jesus.

Third, the miracles of Jesus were performed over a period of time and involved a great variety of powers. He had power over nature, as when He turned the water to wine; He had power over disease, as when he healed the lepers and the blind; He had power over demons, as was shown by His casting them out; He had supernatural powers of knowledge, as in His knowing that Nathaniel was under a fig tree; He demonstrated His power of creation when He fed 5,000 people from a few loaves and fish; and He exhibited power over death itself in the raising of Lazarus and others.

Fourth, we have the testimony of the cured. As noted earlier, we have it from those, like Lazarus, whose healings could not possibly have been psychosomatic or the result of inaccurate diagnosis.

Fifth, we cannot discount the Gospel miracles because of the extravagant claim of pagan miracles. "Miracles are believed in non-Christian religions because the religion is already believed, but in the Biblical religion, miracles are part of the means of establishing the true religion. This distinction is of immense importance. Israel was brought into existence by a series of miracles, the Law was given surrounded by supernatural wonders, and many of the prophets were identified as God's spokesmen by their power to perform miracles. Jesus came not only preaching but performing miracles, and the apostles from time to time worked wonders. It was the miracle authenticating the religion at every point."[4]

As C. S. Lewis writes, "All the essentials of Hinduism would, I think, remain unimpaired if you subtracted the miraculous, and the same is almost true of Muhammadanism, but you cannot do that with Christianity. It is precisely the story of a great Miracle. A naturalistic Christianity leaves out all that is specifically Christian."[5]

Miracles recorded outside the Bible do not display the same order, dignity and motive as those in Scripture. But what is more important, they do not have the same solid authentication as the Biblical miracles. We have discussed at some length the historical reliability of Bible records. Similar investigations into pagan records of miracles would soon show there is no basis for comparison. The same could be said of many so-called miracles and alleged healings of our own time. They do not stand the full weight of investigation. But to take some ancient pagan miracle, or a contemporary claim, and to show their great improbability is not fair to Biblical miracles. The fact that some miracles are counterfeits is no proof that *all* are spurious, any more than the discovery of some counterfeit currency would prove all currency spurious.

---

[4]Ibid., *pp. 142, 143.*
[5]Lewis, C. S. Miracles, *p. 83. New York: Macmillan, 1947; quoted by Ramm in* op. cit.

Some attempts have been made to explain miracles on the basis of exaggerated reporting. It has been demonstrated that people are notoriously inaccurate in reporting events and impressions. Playing the simple parlor game of Rumor is enough to confirm this fact. In the light of this tendency, we are told, it is obvious that the reliability of a human being as an observer may be severely questioned. Consequently, we can discount the Gospel accounts of miracles as the mistaken observations of inaccurate observers.

It may be answered that despite this tendency, law courts have not ceased functioning, and eyewitnesses are still considered able to provide highly useful information. And though there may be some question about such details of an accident as the time, speed of the cars, etc., the accident cannot be said not to have happened because of discrepancies in witnesses' stories. As Ramm observes, the smashed cars and the injured people are irrefutable evidence on which all agreed.[6] We must be careful to see the limitations of arguments such as the unreliability of witnesses. It will help us greatly to see that some of these arguments, pressed to their outer limits, refute the very assertions they set out to make. For instance, those conducting the experiments to establish the unreliability of human witnesses must assume their own reliability or they will have to throw out their own conclusions as being the result of human observation, which is unreliable!

Another erroneus idea, sometimes advanced, is that the miracle stories must be discarded because they are told by believing disciples and are therefore not "objective." But the disciples were the

[6]*Ramm. Op. cit., p. 160.*

ones on the scene who saw the miracles. The fact that they were disciples is neither here nor there. The question is, Did they tell the truth? As we have seen, eyewitness testimony is the best we can get, and most of the disciples faced the test of death as the test of their veracity.

We would not today, in a court of law, say that in order to guarantee objectivity on the part of witnesses, we will listen only to those who were not at the scene of an accident and had nothing to do with it. Nor would we say we would not take testimony from eyewitnesses, including the victims, because they would be "prejudiced." The crucial question in each case is truthfulness, not proximity or relationship to the events.

We have seen that the question of whether miracles are possible is not scientific, but philosophical. Science can only say miracles do not occur in the ordinary course of nature. Science cannot "forbid" miracles because natural laws do not cause, and therefore cannot forbid, anything. They are merely descriptions of what happens. The Christian embraces the concept of natural law. "It is essential to the theistic doctrine of miracles that nature be uniform in her daily routine. If nature were utterly spontaneous, miracles would be as impossible of detection as it would be to establish a natural law.'"

It is "scientism," rather than science, which says miracles cannot happen. The scientist, like anyone else, can only ask, "Are the records of miracles historically reliable?"

Further, we have seen the miracles in the Bible are an inherent part of God's communication to us—not a mere appendage of little significance. We

---

'Ibid., *p. 40.*

have seen that the whole question ultimately depends on the existence of God. Settle that question and miracles cease to be a problem. The very uniformity against which a miracle stands in stark contrast depends on an omnipotent Author of natural law who is also capable of transcending it to accomplish His sovereign ends.

CHAPTER 9

DO SCIENCE
AND SCRIPTURE CONFLICT?

IF EVER THERE WAS a question the attempted answer to which has generated more heat than light,
this is it. Most of the apparent conflict stems from
making the Bible say things it really does not say
and from "scientism," a philosophic interpretation
of facts. These interpretations are distinct from the
facts themselves.

To the question, "Have some scientists and some
Christians conflicted?" the answer would have to
be a resounding "Yes!" We need only recall the
Church's persecution of Galileo, the famous Scopes
trial of 1925, or the unfortunate confrontation, a
century ago, between Bishop Wilberforce and T. H.
Huxley, to know that this is the case.

Part of the problem, as we have indicated, stems
from some well-meaning but misguided Christians
who make the Bible say what it does not say. One
classic and harmful example is the Bible chronology which was calculated by Bishop James Ussher
(1581-1656), a contemporary of Shakespeare. He
worked out a series of dates from the genealogies in
the Bible and concluded that the world was created in 4004 B.C.

It is thought by many non-Christians, including the famous Lord Bertrand Russell, that Fundamentalists actually believe creation occurred in 4004 B.C. Some time ago I was visiting a non-Christian student on a Midwestern state university campus. He picked up a true-false exam in a course on Western Civilization. One question read, "According to the Bible, the world was created in 4004 B.C." "I suppose your instructor wants you to mark this question true," I said. "That's right," the student replied. "Interesting," I mused. Pulling an Oxford edition of the Bible from my pocket, I said, "I wonder if you could show me where the Bible says that." The student was puzzled that he couldn't immediately find the date on the first page of Genesis. Trying to be helpful, the Christian student who was with me volunteered, "It's on page 3." It was news to both of them that Bishop Ussher's dates, which appear in many (but not *all*) English Bibles, are not part of the text.

On the other hand, some scientists are given to making statements that go beyond the facts. These statements are, in fact, philosophic interpretations of data which do not carry the same weight of authority as the data themselves. Unfortunately, the facts and the interpretations are seldom distinguished in the minds of listeners.

When a scientist speaks on *any* subject, he is likely to be believed. He may be speaking outside his field, but the same respect that should rightfully be given to his statements from *within* his field are almost unconsciously transferred to *everything* he says. For instance, Anthony Standen quotes R. S. Lull, professor of paleontology at Yale, as saying, "Since Darwin's day, evolution has been more and more generally accepted, until now, in the minds of informed thinking men, there is no doubt that it is the only logical way whereby creation can be interpreted and understood. We are not so sure as to the *modus operandi*, but we may rest assured that the process has been in accordance with great natural laws, some of which are as yet unknown and are perhaps unknowable."[1]

But one may be tempted to ask, If some of the great natural laws are as yet unknown, how do we know they are there? And if some of them are perhaps unknowable, how do we know they are "logical?"

If we limit ourselves to what the Bible actually says and to what the scientific facts actually are, we shrink the area of controversy enormously. It should be noted here that as Christians we must realize that there may be honest differences of opinion among equally orthodox and committed Christians as to what the Bible means in some instances—for instance, the meaning of "day" in Genesis 1. We must be slow to condemn as a heretic someone whose interpretation of a particular passage may differ from ours. As long as one agrees that what the Bible teaches is authoritative, he is within the bounds of orthodoxy. It is when one admits the Bible is teaching something clearly, like a historic Adam (cf. Rom. 5) but does *not accept* it, that he has crossed the line of Biblical orthodoxy.

Another area in which conflict has arisen is on the question of whether those things which cannot be verified by the scientific method are valid and real. Some people consciously, and others unconsciously, assume that if a statement cannot be proved in a laboratory by the methods of natural

---

[1]*Standen, Anthony.* Science Is a Sacred Cow, *p. 106. New York: E. P. Dutton, 1962, quoting R. S. Lull,* Organic Evolution *(Macmillan, 1947).*

science, it is untrustworthy and cannot be accepted as reliable. The findings of science are considered to be objective and therefore real; statements that must be accepted by faith are looked upon as suspect.

But there are ways and means other than the laboratory to acquire real and genuine knowledge. Consider the process of falling in love. This surely is not done in a laboratory, with a battery of instruments, but anyone who has ever experienced it would be the last to admit that his knowledge of love is uncertain or unreal. We have seen earlier that the scientific method is valid only for those realities which are measurable in physical terms. God is a different kind of reality from the world of nature which science examines. God does not await man's empirical investigation; He is a personal Being who has revealed Himself in love and can be known in personal presence.

Faith is no detriment to the apprehension of reality. In fact, science itself rests on presuppositions which must be accepted by faith before research is possible. One such assumption is that the universe is orderly, that it operates according to a pattern, and that therefore one can predict its behavior.

It should be observed here that the scientific method, as we know it today, began in the sixteenth century among men who were Christians. Breaking with the Greek polytheistic concepts which viewed the universe as capricious and irregular, and therefore not capable of systematic study, they reasoned that the universe must be orderly and worthy of investigation because it was the work of an intelligent Creator. In pursuing scientific research, they were convinced they were thinking God's thoughts after Him.

Another unprovable presupposition that must be

accepted by faith is the reliability of our sense perceptions. One must believe that our senses are trustworthy enough to get a true picture of the universe and enable us to understand the orderliness we observe.

Christians, then, believe that science is one avenue to the discovery of truth about physical things, but that there are other nonmaterial realities and other means of attaining truth. A Christian exercises faith and has presuppositions, as does a scientist, and in this he sees nothing incompatible with reason or intelligence. It is apparent that there are many Christians who are scientists. They do not consider themselves intellectual schizophrenics, but rather view themselves as following in the footsteps of the Christian founders of modern science.

It should further be recognized that science is incapable of making value judgments about the things it measures. Many men on the frontiers of science are realizing that there is nothing inherent in science to guide them in the application of the discoveries they make. There is nothing in science itself which will determine whether nuclear energy will be used to destroy cities or destroy cancer. This is a judgment outside the scientific method to determine.

Further, science can tell us how something works but not *why* it works that way. Whether there is any purpose in the universe can never be answered for us by science. As one writer put it, "Science can give us the 'know-how,' but it cannot give us the 'know-why.' "[2]

We are dependent on revelation for many kinds of information, the absence of which leaves us with a quite incomplete picture. The Bible does not pur-

---

[2]*Hawthorne.* Op. cit., *p. 4.*

port to tell us the *how* of many things, but it clearly gives us the *why*'s.

This is not to say that when the Scriptures refer to matters of science and history they are inaccurate, but rather to point out the focus of their attention.

Humility, then is a valuable virtue for a non-Christian scientist and for a Christian, be he scientist or not. Incalculable harm has been done by the use of argument by ridicule. A sarcastic remark is always good for a long loud laugh from some of the faithful, but invariably it loses the thoughtful person, wavering in his conviction, and the timid unbeliever making his first tentative investigation.

Some have erroneously thought that God was necessary to explain areas of life and existence for which at the moment there was no other explanation. Unbelieving scientists seize on this concept to point out that these gaps are narrowing. "Give us enough time," they say, "and man will be able to explain how everything in the universe works."

Those who adopt this point of view forget that God is not only Creator, but also Sustainer. "He is before all things, and by Him all things consist" (Col. 1:17). The universe would fall apart without His sustaining power. Even if man understands and explains everything, he will still need God. Knowing how the universe is sustained is not the same thing as sustaining it.

For instance, there is much talk today about the possibility of scientists creating life in a test tube. (It should be noted that one's definition of life has much to do with how close he thinks he is to the threshold of creating it.) Some earnest Christians fear that should this event take place, God will somehow have been torn from His throne. But what in fact would have happened? What will it prove. Only that life did not come by blind chance, but by an intelligent mind. It will be apparent to even the most simpleminded that this new "life" has not come into being by the random coincidence and interaction of matter, but as a result of prodigious thought and work under the most rigidly controlled conditions. It would clearly argue for theism. And we still must account for the elements used to produce life. Where did *they* come from? The most logical explanation is that God made them. If man can, in fact, think God's thoughts after Him, it should not be so inconceivable that man may be able to bring life out of a test tube— but he has not thereby become God.

Perhaps no greater contemporary battleground is being faced daily by evangelical Christians in educational institutions than the question of evolution. The very word starts the adrenal glands working overtime. Part of the tension arises from casting the problem into black-and-white terms. Many think that either a person believes in total fiat creation or he is a completely agnostic or atheistic evolutionist.

Whenever the term "evolution" is used, however, we should be careful to define what we mean and to ask others, when they use it, to define what they mean. There are many theories on evolution. Ramm has a helpful list.[3]

First there is an anti-Christian, naturalistic brand of theory of evolution. Evolution as a theory has been expanded to fields far outside biology and, in fact, has become for many a philosophy of life which explains history, society, and religion.

[3]*Ramm, Bernard.* The Christian View of Science and Scripture, *p. 261 ff. Grand Rapids: Wm. B. Eerdmans, 1954. His whole discussion is helpful. Some of the material in this chapter is taken from it.*

With this expansion of the theory of evolution into a philosophy of life there is no common ground with evangelical Christianity. We repudiate it completely.

Not all who hold a form of evolution fit into this category, however. There are those who hold it in a spiritual context. The modern Thomistic interpretation of evolution says that evolution is merely the way God chose to work, and that there would be no evolution if there were no God.

Then there is the theory of emergent evolution. Those holding this view believe life and mind appeared miraculously. From original life to mind, life kept emerging on higher and higher levels. The new levels were not reached by chance evolution, but were sudden and novel appearances.

Then there are a few people in the evangelical camp who hold to theistic evolution. They see no conflict between this view and their Christian faith. Among them were such stalwarts as James Orr and A. G. Strong. Most orthodox Catholic theologians also believe in theistic evolution.

The above is merely to show that the alternatives are not fiat creation and atheistic evolution. And in evangelism, it is useless to get into a discussion of evolution. I first ask an evolutionist whether he is concluding from his position that there is no God and that everything happened by chance, or whether he concedes God is the Author of life. If he accepts the latter, I confront him directly with Jesus Christ. *He* is the real issue in salvation, not one's view of evolution. When the issue of Christ is settled, other less important ones settle themselves in due course.

Two extremes must be avoided. First is the assumption that evolution has been proved without doubt and that anyone with a brain in his head must accept it. The second is the notion that evolution is "only a theory," with little evidence for it.

Scientific theory is a matter of the highest degree of probability based on the data available. There are no absolutes in it. Furthermore, science is a train that is constantly moving. Yesterday's generalization is today's discarded hypothesis. This is one reason for being somewhat tentative about accepting any form of evolutionary theory as the final explanation of biology. It is also why it is dangerous to try to "prove" the Bible by science. If the Bible becomes wedded to today's scientific theories, what will happen to it when science, ten years from now, has shifted?

Thoughtful evolutionists are ready to concede that the matter is not an open-and-shut case, but they feel the theory must be accepted despite some seeming contradictions and unexplained factors.

The following is of such interest that I quote it at length to illustrate this point. After discussing how pathetically theology students at Cambridge, in a former century, accepted dogma and teachings they did not fully understand or personally investigate, G. A. Kerkut, an evolutionist, points out that many present-day undergraduates have succumbed to the same unthinking tendencies in their studies in general, and in accepting evolution in biology in particular.

"For some years now (he writes), I have tutored undergraduates on various aspects of biology. It is quite common, during the course of conversation, to ask the student if he knows the evidence for evolution. This usually evokes a faintly superior smile. . . . 'Well, sir, there is the evidence from paleontology, comparative anatomy, embryology, systematics, and geographical distributions,' the student would say in a nursery rhyme jargon, some-

times even ticking off the words on his fingers. He
would then sit and look fairly complacent and wait
or a more difficult question, such as the nature of
the evidence for natural selection. Instead I would
continue on evolution.

" 'Do you think that the evolutionary theory is
the best explanation yet advanced to explain animal interrelationships?' I would ask.

" 'Why, of course, sir,' would be the reply.
'There *is* nothing else, except for the religious explanation held by some Fundamentalist Christians,
and I gather, sir, that these views are no longer
held by the more up-to-date Churchmen.'

" 'So you believe in evolution because there is no
other theory?'

" 'Oh, no, sir, I believe in it because of the evidence I just mentioned.'

" 'Have you read any book on the evidence for
evolution?' I would ask.

" 'Yes, sir.' And here he would mention the
names of authors of a popular school textbook.
'And of course, sir, there is that book by Darwin,
The Origin of Species.'

" 'Have you read this book?' I would ask.

" 'Well, not all through, sir.'

" 'The first 50 pages?'

" 'Yes, sir, about that much; maybe a bit less.'

" 'I see. And that has given you your firm understanding of evolution?'

" 'Yes, sir.'

" 'Well, now, if you really understand an argument you will be able to indicate to me not only
the points in favor of the argument, but also the
most telling points against it.'

" 'I suppose so, sir.'

" 'Good. Please tell me, then, some of the evidence against the theory of evolution.'

110

" 'But there isn't any, sir.'

"Here the conversation would take on a more strained atmosphere. The student would look at me as if I were playing a very unfair game. He would take it rather badly when I suggested that he was not being very scientific in his outlook if he swallowed the latest scientific dogma and, when questioned, just repeated parrot-fashion the views of the current Archbishop of Evolution. In fact he would be behaving like certain of those religious students he affected to despise. He would be taking on faith what he could not intellectually understand and, when questioned, would appeal to authority of a 'good book,' which in this case was *The Origin of Species*. (It is interesting to note that many of these widely quoted books are read by title only. Three of such that come to mind are the Bible, *The Origin of Species*, and *Das Kapital*.)

"I would suggest that the student should go away and read the evidence for and against evolution and present it as an essay. A week would pass and the same student would appear armed with an essay on the evidence for evolution. The essay would usually be well done, since the students might have realized that I should be rough to convince. When the essay had been read and the question concerning the evidence against evolution came up, the student would give a rather pained smile. 'Well, sir, I looked up various books but could not find anything in the scientific books against evolution. I did not think you would want a religious argument.' 'No, you were quite correct. I want a scientific argument against evolution.' 'Well, sir, there does not seem to be one, and that in itself is a piece of evidence in favor of the evolutionary theory.'

"I would then indicate to him that the theory of

111

evolution was of considerable antiquity, and would mention that he might have looked at the book by Radi, *The History of Biological Theories*. Having made sure the student had noted the book down for future reference I would proceed as follows:

" 'Before one can decide that the theory of evolution is the best explanation of the present-day range of forms of living material, one should examine all the implications that such a theory may hold. Too often the theory is applied to, say, the development of the horse, and then, because it is held to be applicable there, it is extended to the rest of the animal kingdom with little or no further evidence.

" 'There are, however, seven basic assumptions that are often not mentioned during discussions of evolution. Many evolutionists ignore the first six assumptions and consider only the seventh.

" 'The first assumption is that nonliving things gave rise to living material, i.e., that spontaneous generation occurred.

" 'The second assumption is that spontaneous generation occurred only once.

" 'The third . . . is that viruses, bacteria, plants, and animals are all interrelated.

" 'The fourth . . . is that the protozoa gave rise to the metazoa.

" 'The fifth . . . is that the various invertebrate phyla are interrelated.

" 'The sixth . . . is that the invertebrates gave rise to the vertebrates.

" 'The seventh . . . is that the vertebrates and fish gave rise to the amphibia, the amphibia to the reptiles, and the reptiles to the birds and mammals. Sometimes this is expressed in other words, i.e., that the modern amphibia and reptiles had a common ancestral stock, and so on.

" 'For the initial purposes of this discussion on evolution I shall consider that the supporters of the theory of evolution hold that all these seven assumptions are valid, and that these assumptions form the general theory of evolution.

" 'The first point that I should like to make is that *the seven assumptions by their nature are not capable of experimental verification*. [Italics mine.] They assume that a certain series of events has occurred in the past. Thus, though it may be possible to mimic some of these events under present-day conditions, this does not mean that these events *must* therefore have taken place in the past. All that it shows is that it is *possible* for such a change to take place. Thus, to change a present-day reptile into a mammal, though of great interest, would not show the way in which the mammals *did* arise. Unfortunately, we cannot bring about even this change; instead we have to depend upon limited circumstantial evidence for our assumptions, and it is now my intention to discuss the nature of this evidence.' "[4]

As Ramm observes, "There as yet remains the proof of the inorganic origin of life. It may be assumed, but it is not yet verified. There is the problem of the rugged species which have endured without change for millions of years. There is the problem of the sudden appearance of new forms in the geologic record."[5] It is erroneous to speak of the missing link. In fact there are thousands of missing links.

There is the further problem of the apparent conflict of the evolutionary theory with the second

---

[4]*Kerkut, G. A. "Implications of Evolution,"* International Series of Monographs of Pure and Applied Biology, *Vol. 4, p. 3. Pergamon Press, 1960.*
[5]*Ramm. Op. cit., p. 273.*

law of thermodynamics. This is also called the law of entropy. It says, in essence, that "in any energy transfer or change, though the total amount of energy remains unchanged, the amount of usefulness and availability that the energy possesses is always decreased."[6] Evolution and entropy are seemingly incompatible. The universe is running down, not building up. As Ramm says, "We are faced clearly with the two theories of (1) the recoverability of energy and (2) the irrecoverability of energy. If energy is irrecoverable we are faced with the doctrine of creation. To this hour no known process of recoverability is proven."[7]

Much of the problem and controversy over evolution hinges on the definition of species. It seems to me that once this is understood a good bit of hassling among evangelicals becomes unnecessary. If we identify species as we know them scientifically today with the term "kind" in Genesis 1, then we have enormous problems when we speak of the fixity of species. But this is an incorrect identification. Even so staunch an antievolutionist as Henry M. Morris says, "It is well to observe . . . that the Bible does not teach the fixity of species, and for this simple reason no one knows just what a species is. There are few issues more alive among biologists today than this matter of what constitutes a species. *Certainly, according to many definitions of the term, many new species have been evolved since the original creation* [italics mine]. Genetic research has proved conclusively that chromosome changes, gene mutation, and hybridization can produce, and in fact, have produced, many distinctly

---

[6]*Morris, Henry.* The Bible and Modern Science, *p. 14. Chicago: Moody Press, 1953.*

[7]*Ramm.* Op. cit., *p. 276.*

114

new varieties in both plants and animals. These varieties are often considered new species, or even genera, by most modern methods of classification.

"However, all evidence thus far in the genetic field seems to prove conclusively that these agencies of change cannot go beyond certain comparatively narrow limits, and can very definitely not produce new kinds. The Genesis account merely says that each created group was to produce 'after its kind,' with no clear indication as to what constitutes a 'kind,' except the implication that different kinds would not be interfertile (if they were, they would not be reproducing after their respective kinds). Thus, the Biblical account leaves ample room for just such conditions of change within the smaller groups, and stability within the larger groups, as is indicated by modern discovery.[8]

In the same vein, Russell Mixter says, "As a creationist I am willing to accept the origin of species from other species, called micro-evolution"[9] He rejects macro-evolution, which would be evolution of everything from one original. Carnell likewise thinks there is a wide possibility of change within the kinds originally created by God. These variations, however, cannot cross certain prescribed boundaries. He says, "Observe therefore that the conservative may scrap the doctrine of the 'fixity of species' also without jeopardizing his major premise in the least."[10]

We reiterate that the so-called conflicts of

[8]*Morris.* Op. cit., *p. 45.*

[9]*Mixter, Russell. "The Science of Heredity and the Source of the Species,"* Creation and Evolution, *p. 2, 1945. Quoted by Ramm,* op. cit., *p. 288.*

[10]*Carnell, E. J.* An Introduction to Christian Apologetics, *p. 238. Quoted by Ramm.* op. cit., *p. 289.*

science and the Bible are often conflicts between interpretations of the facts.

The presupposition one brings to the facts, rather than the facts themselves, determines one's conclusion. For instance, one might be told that his wife was seen riding around town with another man. Knowing his wife, he draws a different conclusion from this fact than does the town gossip. The different conclusions result, not from different facts, but from different presuppositions brought to the fact.

In everything we read and in everything we hear we must ask, "What is this person's presupposition?" so that we may interpret conclusions in this light. There is no such thing as total objectivity, in science or in anything else.

While there are problems for which there is as yet no explanation, there is no fundamental conflict between science and Scripture.

CHAPTER 10

WHY DOES GOD ALLOW SUFFERING AND EVIL?

THIS IS ONE of the most pressing questions of our time. More pressing than the question of miracles or science and the Bible is the poignant problem of why innocent people suffer, why babies are born blind, or why a promising life is snuffed out as it is on the rise. Why are there wars in which thousands of innocent people are killed, children burned beyond recognition, and many maimed for life?

In the classic statement of the problem, either God is all-powerful but not all-good, and therefore doesn't stop evil, or He is all-good but unable to stop evil, in which case He is not all-powerful.

The general tendency is to blame God for evil and suffering and to pass on all responsibility for it to Him.

There are no easy answers to this profound question. It is not one to be treated lightly or in a doctrinaire fashion. We might paraphrase a famous expression, "They ignore scars who never felt a wound." But there are some factors which should be kept in mind.

We must never forget that when God created man, He created him perfect. Man was not created

117

evil. He did, however, as a human being, have ability to obey or disobey God. Had man obeyed God there would never have been a problem. He would have lived an unending life of fellowship with God and enjoyment of Him and His creation. This is what God intended for man when He created him. In fact, however, the first man rebelled against God—and every one of us has ratified that rebellion. "Wherefore as by one man sin entered into the world, and death by sin, and so death passed upon all men, for that all have sinned" (Rom. 5:12). The point we must keep in mind is that *man* is responsible for sin—not God.

But many ask, Why didn't God make us so we couldn't sin? To be sure, He *could* have, but let's remember that if He had done so we would no longer be human beings, we would be machines. How would you like to be married to a chatty doll? Every morning and every night you could pull the string and get the beautiful words, "I love you." There would never be any hot words, never any conflict, never anything said or done that would make you sad! But who would want that? There would never be any love, either. Love is voluntary. God could have made us like robots, but we would have ceased to be men. God apparently thought it worth the risk of creating us as we are. In any case He did it and we must face the realities.

We must also recognize that God could stamp out evil if He chose. Jeremiah reminds us, "It is of the Lord's mercies that we are not consumed, because His compassions fail not" (Lam. 3:22). A time is coming when He will stamp out evil in the world. The devil and all his works will come under eternal judgment. In the meantime, God's love and grace prevail and His offer of mercy and pardon is still open.

If God were to stamp out evil today, He would do a *complete* job. But we want Him to stop war but to stay remote from us. If God were to remove evil from the universe, His action would be complete and would have to include our lies and personal impurities, our lack of love, and our failure to do good. Suppose God were to decree that at midnight tonight *all* evil would be removed from the universe—who of us would still be here after midnight?

And God *has* done something about the problem of evil. He has done the most dramatic, costly, and effective thing possible by giving His Son to die for evil men. It is possible for man to escape God's inevitable judgment on sin and evil. It is also possible to have its power broken by entering into a personal relationship with the Lord Jesus Christ. The ultimate answer to the problem of evil, at the personal level is found in the sacrificial death of Jesus Christ.

To speculate about the origin of evil is endless. No one has the full answer. It belongs in the category of "the secret things [that] belong unto the Lord our God" (Deut. 29:29).

We are faced with the stark reality of the fact of evil, and it is with this reality that we must grapple.

Part of our problem arises from our limited definition of the word *good* and our applying this term to God. Hugh Evan Hopkins observes, "In his famous essay on Nature, John Stuart Mill clearly sets out the problem with which thinkers all through history have wrestled: If the law of all creation were justice and the Creator omnipotent, then in whatever amount suffering and happiness might be dispensed to the world, each person's share would be exactly proportioned to that person's good or evil deeds. No human being would

119

have a worse lot than another without worse deserts; accident or favoritism would have no part in such a world, but every human life would be playing out a drama constructed like a perfect moral tale. Not even on the most distorted and contracted theory of good which ever was framed by religious or philosophical fanaticism can the government of nature be made to resemble the work of a being at once both good and omnipotent."[1]

"The problem arises largely from the belief that a 'good' God would reward each man according to his deserts and that an 'almighty' God would have no difficulty in carrying this out. The fact that rewards and punishments, in the way of happiness and discomfort, appear to be haphazardly distributed in this life drives many to question either the goodness of God or His power."[2]

But would God be good if He were to deal with each person exactly according to his behavior? Consider what this would mean in your own life! The whole of the Gospel as previewed in the Old Testament and broadcast in stereo-television in the New Testament is that God's goodness consists not *only* in His justice but also in His love, mercy and kindness. How thankful we and all men should be that "He hath not dealt with us after our sins; nor rewarded us according to our iniquities. For as the heaven is high above the earth, so great is His mercy toward them that fear Him" (Ps. 103:10, 11).

Such a concept of the goodness of God is also based on the faulty assumption that happiness is the greatest good in life. Happiness is usually

[1]*Hopkins, Hugh Evan.* Mystery of Suffering. *Chicago: Inter-Varsity Press, 1959. Quoting J. S. Mill,* Essays, *p. 38.*
[2]Ibid., *p. 13.*

thought of in terms of comfort. True, genuine, deep-seated happiness, however, is something much more profound than the ephemeral fleeting enjoyment of the moment. And true happiness is not precluded by suffering. Sometimes, in His infinite wisdom, God knows that there are things to be accomplished in our character that can be brought only through suffering. To shield us from this suffering would be to rob us of a greater good. Peter refers to this when he says, "But the God of all grace, who hath called us unto His eternal glory by Christ Jesus, after that ye have suffered awhile, make you perfect, stablish, strengthen, settle you" (I Pet. 5:10).

To see the logical consequence of Mill's "exact reward" concept of God in His dealings with us, we need only turn to Hinduism. The law of Karma says that all of the actions of life today are the result of the actions of a previous life. Blindness, poverty, hunger, physical deformity, outcastness, and other social agonies are all the outworking of punishment for evil deeds in a previous existence. It would follow that any attempt to alleviate such pain and misery would be an interference with the just ways of God. This concept is one reason why the Hindus did so little for so long for their unfortunates. Some enlightened Hindus today are talking about and working toward social progress and change, but they have not yet reconciled this new concept with the clear, ancient doctrine of Karma, which is basic to Hindu thought and life.

This Karma concept, however, *does* serve as a neat, simple, clearly understood explanation of suffering: suffering is all the result of previous evildoing.

But is there not a sense in which it is true that

121

Christianity also holds that suffering is punishment from God?

Certainly, in the minds of many, it is. "What did I do to deserve this?" is often the first question on the lips of a sufferer. And the conviction of friends, expressed or unexpressed, frequently operates on this same assumption. The classic treatment of the problem of suffering and evil in the Book of Job shows how this cruel assumption was accepted by Job's friends. It compounded his already staggering pain.

It is clear from the teaching of both the Old and the New Testaments that suffering *may* be the judgment of God, but that there are many instances when it is totally unrelated to personal wrongdoing. An automatic assumption of guilt and consequent punishment is totally unwarranted.

To be sure, God is not a sentimental, beard-stroking, grandfather of the sky with a "boys-will-be-boys" attitude. "Whatsoever a man soweth, that shall he also reap" (Gal. 6:7) is a solemn warning to any who would tweak God's nose in arrogant presumption. God afflicted Miriam with leprosy for challenging the authority of Moses, her brother, whom God had appointed leader. He took the life of David's child, born of his adulterous relationship with Bathsheba. Other examples could be cited. In the New Testament we have the startling example of Ananias and Sapphira, who were struck dead for lying, cheating, and hypocrisy. That there may be a connection between suffering and sin is evident, but that it is not always so is abundantly clear. We have the unambiguous word of our Lord Himself on the subject. The disciples apparently adhered to the direct retribution theory of suffering. One day when they saw a man who had been blind from birth, they wanted to know who had sinned to cause this blindness—the man or his parents. Jesus made it clear that neither was responsible for his condition, "but that the works of God should be made manifest in him" (John 9:1-3).

On receiving word of some Galileans whom Pilate had slaughtered, Jesus went out of his way to point out that they were not greater sinners than other Galileans. He said the 18 people killed when the tower of Siloam fell on them were not greater sinners than others in Jerusalem. From both incidents He made the point, "Except ye repent, ye shall all likewise perish" (Luke 13:1-3).

Clearly, then, we are jumping the gun if we assume automatically, either in our own case or in that of another, that the explanation of any given tragedy or suffering is the judgment of God. Further, as Hopkins observes, it seems clear from Biblical examples that if one's troubles are the just rewards of misdeeds, the sufferer is never left in any doubt when his trouble is a punishment.

Indeed, one of the profound truths of the whole of Scripture is that the judgment of God is preceded by warning. Throughout the Old Testament we have the repeated pleadings of God and warning of judgment. Only after warning is persistently ignored and rejected does judgment come. God's poignant words are an example: "I have no pleasure in the death of the wicked . . . turn ye, turn ye from your evil ways, for why will ye die, O house of Israel?" (Ezek. 33:11).

The same theme continues in the New Testament. What more moving picture of God's love and long-suffering is there than our Lord as He weeps over Jerusalem, "O Jerusalem, Jerusalem . . . how often would I have gathered thy children together, even as a hen gathereth her chickens under her wings, and ye would not!" (Matt. 23:37) And we have the clear word of Peter that "the Lord is . . . not willing that any should perish but that all should come to repentance" (II Pet. 3:9).

When the question, "How could a good God send people to hell?" comes up, we should point out that, in a sense, God sends no one to hell. Each person sends himself. God has done all that is necessary for us to be forgiven, redeemed, cleansed, and made fit for heaven. All that remains is for us to receive this gift. If we refuse it, God has no option but to give us our choice. Heaven, for the person who does not want to be there, would be hell.

Though the judgment of God sometimes explains suffering, there are several other possibilities to consider. Man, as we saw earlier, was responsible for the coming of sin and death into the universe. We must not forget that his wrongdoing is also responsible for a great deal of misery and suffering in the world today. Negligence in the construction of a building has sometimes resulted in its collapse in a storm, with consequent death and injury. How many lives have been snuffed out by the murder of drunken driving? The cheating, lying, stealing, and selfishness which are so characteristic of our society today all reap a bitter harvest of suffering. But we can hardly blame God for it! Think of all the misery that has its origin in the wrongdoing of man—it is remarkable how much suffering is accounted for in this way.

But man is not alone on this planet. By divine revelation we know of the presence of an enemy. He appears in various forms, we are told, appropriate to the occasion. He may appear as an angel of light or is a roaring lion, depending on the circumstances and his purposes. His name is Satan. It was he whom God allowed to cause Job to suffer.

Jesus, in the parable of the good seed and the tares, explains the ruining of the farmer's harvest by saying, "An enemy hath done this" (Matt. 13:28). Satan finds great pleasure in ruining God's creation and causing misery and suffering. God allows him limited power, but he cannot touch the one in close fellowship with God. "Resist the devil and he will flee from you" (James 4:7), we are assured. Nevertheless Satan accounts for some of the disease and suffering in the world today.

In answer to the question of why God allows Satan power to bring suffering, we can learn from Robinson Crusoe's answer to his Man Friday. "Well," says Friday, "you say God is so strong, so great; has He not as much strong, as much might as the devil?" "Yes, yes," says I; "Friday, God is much stronger than the devil." "But if God much strong, much might as the devil, why God no kill the devil so make him no more do wicked?" "You may as well ask," answers Crusoe reflectively, "Why does God not kill you and me when we do wicked things that offend Him?"

In considering pain and suffering, whether it be physical or mental, another important consideration must be kept in mind. God is not a distant, aloof, impervious potentate, far removed from His people and their sufferings. He not only is aware of suffering—He *feels* it. No pain or suffering has ever come to us that has not first passed through the heart and hand of God. However greatly we may suffer, it is well to remember that God is the great Sufferer. Comforting are the words of Isaiah the prophet, foretelling the agony of Christ: "He is despised and rejected of men, a Man of sorrows and acquainted with grief" (Isa. 53:3). The writer of Hebrews reminds us, "For in that He himself hath suffered being tempted, He is able to succor them that are tempted" (Heb. 2:18). And "We have not a High Priest which cannot be touched with the feeling of our infirmities, but was in all points tempted like as we are, yet without sin" (Heb. 4:15).

The problem of evil and suffering is one of the profound problems of the ages. It is becoming increasingly acute in our time, with the advent of The Bomb. There are no easy answers, and we do not have the last word. There are, however, clues.

First, as J. B. Phillips has put it, "Evil is inherent in the risky gift of free will."[3] God could have made us machines, but to do so would have robbed us of our precious freedom of choice, and we would have ceased to be human. Exercise of free choice in the direction of evil, in what we call the "fall" of man, is the basic reason for evil and suffering in the world. It is man's responsibility, not God's. He could stop it, but in so doing would destroy us all. It is worth noting "that the whole point of real Christianity lies not in interference with the human power to choose, but in producing a willing consent to choose good rather than evil."[4]

Unless the universe is without significance, the actions of every individual affect others. No man is an island. To have it otherwise would be like playing a game of chess and changing the rules after every move. Life would be meaningless.

Second, much of the suffering in the world can be traced directly to the evil choices men and women make. This is quite apparent when a hold-up man kills someone. Sometimes it is less apparent and more indirect, as when crooked decisions

---

[3]*Phillips, J. B.* **God Our Contemporary**, *p. 88. New York: Macmillan, 1960.*
[4]*Ibid. p. 89.*

are made in government or business that may bring deprivation and suffering to many people unknown to those who make the decisions. Even the results of natural disasters are sometimes compounded by man's culpability in refusing to heed warnings of tidal waves, volcanic eruptions, floods, etc.

Third, some—but not all—suffering is allowed by God as judgment and punishment. This is a possibility which must always be considered. God usually allows such suffering —with a view to restoration and character formation, and those suffering as a result of their deeds usually know it.

Fourth, God has an implacable enemy in Satan. He has been defeated at the Cross, but is free to work his evil deeds until the final judgment. That there is in the world a force of evil stronger than man himself is clear from revelation and from experience.

Fifth, God Himself is the great Sufferer and has fully met the problem of evil in the gift of His own Son, at infinite cost to Himself. The consequence of evil for eternity is forever removed as we embrace the Lord Jesus Christ. Our sin is forgiven and we receive new life and power to *choose* what is right as the Holy Spirit forms the image of Christ in us.

Perhaps the greatest test of faith for the Christian today is to believe that God is good. There is so much which, taken in isolation, suggests the contrary. Helmut Thielecke of Hamburg points out that a fabric viewed through a magnifying glass is clear in the middle and blurred at the edges. But we know the edges are clear because of what we see in the middle. Life, he says, is like a fabric. There are many edges which are blurred, many events and circumstances we do not understand. But they are to be interpreted by the clarity we see in the center—the cross of Christ. We are not left to guess about the goodness of God from isolated bits of data. He has clearly revealed His character and dramatically demonstrated it to us in the Cross. "He that spared not His own Son, but delivered Him up for us all, how shall He not with Him also freely give us all things?" (Rom. 8:32)

God never asks us to understand; we need only trust Him in the same way we ask that our child only trust *our* love, though we may not understand or appreciate our taking him to the doctor.

Peace comes when we realize we are able to see only a few threads in the grand tapestry of life and God's will, and that we do not have the full picture.

Then we can affirm, with calm relief and joy, that "all things work together for good to them that love God, to them who are the called according to His purpose" (Rom. 8:28).

At times it is our reaction to suffering, rather than the suffering itself, that determines whether the experience is one of blessing or of blight. The same sun melts the butter and hardens the clay.

When by God's grace we can view all of life through the lens of faith in God's love, we can affirm with Habakkuk, "Although the fig tree shall not blossom, neither shall fruit be in the vines; the labor of the olive shall fail, and the fields shall yield no meat; the flock shall be cut off from the fold, and there shall be no herd in the stalls: yet I will rejoice in the Lord, I will joy in the God of my salvation" (Hab. 3:17, 18).

CHAPTER 11

DOES CHRISTIANITY DIFFER FROM OTHER WORLD RELIGIONS?

THIS QUESTION IS asked frequently in our shrinking modern world. There is, currently, a meeting of cultures, nations, races, and religions on a scale unprecedented in history. In this jet age we are no more than 24 hours away from any spot on the earth. Television brings the coronation of a pope, the burning of a Buddhist monk, and a Muslim ceremony conducted by a political leader into our living rooms.

Almost 100,000 students from more than 150 countries of the world come to the United States every year to study in more than 2,000 colleges and universities in every one of the 5 states. Brightly colored saris on graceful Indian women and striking turbans on erect Sikhs are not unfamiliar sights in our metropolitan areas or small college towns. In addition, there are multiplied thousands of diplomatic, business, and tourist visitors every year.

Many of these visitors find their way into Parent-Teacher Association meetings, service clubs, and churches to speak on their cultural and religious backgrounds. They are sincere, educated, and intelligent. They are often interested in learning about Christianity, and we may learn from them. (Anyone wishing to become acquainted with a foreign student may contact the foreign student advisor on the nearest college or university campus. A free booklet giving practical suggestions on contact and witness may be had by writing the author, c/o Scripture Press, 1825 College Ave., Wheaton, Illinois 60187. Ask for the booklet, *A Guide to International Friendship*.)

As one has contact with these friends from overseas and becomes aware of their religious beliefs, the question naturally arises as to whether or not Christianity is unique among world religions. Or is it only a variation on a basic theme running through all religions? To put it another way, "Does not the sincere Muslim, Buddhist, Hindu or Jew worship the same God as we do, but under a different name?" Or, quite bluntly, "Is Jesus Christ the *only* way to God?"

In answering this question, it is extremely important that we first empty it of its potentially explosive emotional content. When a Christian asserts that Jesus Christ is the only way to God, and that apart from Him there is no salvation, he is not suggesting that he thinks he is, or that Christians in general think they are, better than anyone else. Some people erroneously view Christians as having formed a bigoted club, like a fraternity with a racial segregation clause. If only the fraternity and the Christians were less bigoted, such people think, they would vote to change their membership rules and, in the case of the Christians, let in anyone who believes in God. "Why bring Jesus Christ into it?" we are often asked. "Why can't we just agree on God?" And this brings us to the fundamental issue.

Christians assert that Jesus Christ is the only way to God because Scripture says, "There is none other name under heaven given among men whereby we must be saved" (Acts 4:12). Christians believe this, not because they have made it *their* rule, but because Jesus Christ our Lord taught it (John 14:6). A Christian cannot be faithful to his Lord and affirm anything else. He is faced with the problem of truth. If Jesus Christ is who He claims to be, then we have the authoritative word of God Himself on the subject. If He is God and there is no other Saviour, then obviously He is the *only* way to God. Christians could not change this fact by a vote or by anything else.

It is helpful to point out, to those who ask this question, that there are some laws the penalty for which is socially determined. There are other laws of which this is not true. For instance, the penalty for driving through a stop light is determined by society. It is not inherent in the act itself. The penalty could be set at $25 or at $5, or it could be abolished completely.

With the law of gravity, however, the penalty for violation is not socially determined. People could vote unanimously to suspend the law of gravity for an hour, but no one in his right mind would jump off the roof to test it! No, the penalty for violating that law is inherent in the act itself, and the person who violated it would be picked up with a blotter despite the unanimous resolution!

As there are inherent physical laws, so there are inherent spiritual laws. One of them is God's revelation of Himself in Christ. Another is Christ's death as the only atonement for sin.

In proclaiming the exclusiveness of Christ, a Christian does not assume a superior posture. He speaks as a sinner saved by grace. As D. T. Niles,

131

of Ceylon, so beautifully put it, "Evangelism is just one beggar telling another beggar where to find food."

After defusing the emotional bomb, it is then important to move on to the important question of truth. Sincerely believing something does not make it true, as anyone will testify who has ever picked a wrong bottle out of a medicine cabinet in the dark. Faith is no more valid than the object in which it is placed, no matter how sincere or how intense the faith is. A nurse very sincerely put carbolic acid instead of silver nitrate in the eyes of a newborn baby. Her sincerity did not save the baby from blindness.

These same principles apply to things spiritual. Believing something doesn't make it true any more than failing to believe truth makes it false. Facts are facts, regardless of people's attitudes toward them. In religious matters, the basic question is always, Is it true?

Take, for instance, the fact of the deity, death, and resurrection of the Lord Jesus Christ. Christianity affirms these facts as the heart of its message. Islam, on the other hand, denies the deity, death and resurrection of Christ. On this very crucial point, one of these mutually contradictory views is wrong. They can't simultaneously be true, no matter how sincerely both are believed by how many people.

A great deal is said about the similarity of world religions. Many Christians naively assume that other religions are basically the same, making the same claims and essentially doing what Christianity does, but in slightly different terms. Such an attitude reveals complete ignorance of other religions.

Though there are some similarities, the differences far outweigh, and are much greater than, the similarities.

One of the similarities is the essence of the Golden Rule, which is contained in almost every religion. From Confucius' time we have the statement, in various forms, that one should do unto others as he would have others do unto him. Many wrongly assume that this is the essence of Christianity. But if all Jesus Christ did was to give us the Sermon on the Mount and the Golden Rule, He actually increased our frustration. As we have already seen, man has had the Golden Rule since Confucius' time. Man's problem has never been not knowing what he should do. His problem, rather, has been that he lacks power to do what he knows he should.

Christ raised the ethical level and thereby made the requirements higher. This by itself raises our frustration level. But that is not *all* Christ did, and this is a major difference between Christianity and other religions. Christ offers us His power to live as we should. He gives us forgiveness, cleansing, and His own righteousness, all as a free gift. He reconciles us to God. He does something for us we cannot do for ourselves.

Every other religious system, however, is essentially a do-it-yourself proposition. Follow this way of life, they say, and you will gain favor with God and eventually achieve salvation. In a sense, other religious systems are sets of swimming instructions for a drowning man. Christianity is a life-preserver.

D. T. Niles has also observed that in other religions good works are an "in order to." In Christianity, they are a "therefore." In other religions, good works are the means by which one hopes to earn salvation. In Christianity salvation is received as a free gift, through the finished work of Christ, the "therefore" of good works becomes an imperative love of God. Or, as another has put it, other religions are "do"; Christianity is "done."

Christianity is what God has done for man in seeking Him and reaching down to help him. Other religons are a matter of man seeking and struggling toward God.

Because of this profound difference, Christianity alone offers *assurance* of salvation. Because our salvation depends on what God has done for and given us, we can say with the same wonderful certainty of the Apostle Paul, "To be absent from the body is to be present with the Lord" (II Cor. 5:8).

In every "works" religion, however, it is impossible ever to have assurance. When do you know that you have done enough good works? You *never* know, and never *can* know. Fear persists because there is no assurance of salvation.

What salvation is, and what we are pointing toward, is quite different in the world's religions from what it is in Christianity.

In Buddhism, for instance, the ultimate goal is nirvana, or the extinction of desire. According to Buddha's teaching, all pain and suffering come from *desire*. If this desire can be overcome by following the Eightfold Path to Enlightenment, one can achieve nirvana, which is total nothingness. It is likened to the snuffing out of a candle. This is what is supposed to happen to life and consciousness when nirvana has been achieved.

In Hinduism the ultimate goal is also nirvana, but the term here has a different meaning. Nirvana is ultimate reunion with Brahm, the all-pervading force of the universe which is the Hindu's God. This experience is likened to the return of a drop of water to the ocean. Individuality is lost in the reunion with God, but without the total self-annihilation of Buddhism. Nirvana, in Hinduism, is achieved through a continuous cycle of birth, life, death, and rebirth. As soon as any animal, insect, or human being dies, it or he is immediately reborn in another form. Whether one moves up or down the scale of life depends on the quality of moral life one has lived. If it has been a good life, one moves up the scale with more comfort and less suffering. If one has lived a bad life, he moves down the scale into suffering and poverty. If he has been bad enough he is not reborn as a human being at all, but as an animal or insect. This law of reaping in the next life the harvest of one's present life is called the law of Karma. It explains why Hindus will not kill even an insect, not to mention a sacred cow, though these inhibitions pose grave sanitation and public health problems. What seems strange, curious, and even ludicrous to us of the western world has a very clear rationale to the Hindu, and to us once we understand his thinking.

In Islam, heaven is a paradise of wine, women, and song. It is achieved by living a life in which, ironically, one abstains from the things with which he will be rewarded in paradise. In addition to this abstention, one must follow the Five Pillars of Islam: repeating the creed, making a pilgrimage to Mecca, giving alms to the poor, praying five times daily, and keeping the fast of the month of Ramadan.

Again, there is no possibility of assurance. I have often asked Hindus, Muslims, and Buddhists whether they would achieve nirvana or go to paradise when they died. I have not yet had one reply in the affirmative. Rather, they referred to the imperfection of their lives as being a barrier to this realization. There is no assurance in their religious systems because there is no atonement and because salvation depends on the individual's gaining enough merit.

Even the fundamental concept of God, on which there is a plea that we should agree, reveals wide divergences. To say that we can unite with all who believe in God, regardless of what this God is called, fails to recognize that the term God means nothing apart from the definition given it.

Buddha, contrary to popular belief, never claimed to be deity. In fact, he was agnostic about the whole question of whether God even existed. If God existed, the Buddha taught emphatically, He could not help an individual achieve enlightenment. Each person must work this out for himself.

Hindus are pantheistic. *Pan* means "all" and *theistic* means "God." Hindus believe that God and the universe are identical. The concept of "maya" is central to their thinking. Maya means that the material world is an illusion and that reality is spiritual and invisible. Brahm is the impersonal, all-pervading force of the universe, and the ultimate goal is for man to be reunited with this "God" in nirvana. Buddhism also teaches that the material world is an illusion. It is readily apparent why modern science came to birth through Christians, who believed in a personal God and an orderly universe, rather than in the context of Oriental philosophy. It is clear why most scientific progress has come from the West rather than the East. Why would one investigate what he believes is an illusion?

In Islam and Judaism we have a God much closer to the Christian concept. Here God is personal and transcendent, or separate from His creation. Surely, we are urged, we may get together with those who believe in God in personal terms.

But as we examine the Muslim concept of God—

"Allah," as He is called in the *Koran*—we find he is not the God and Father of our Lord Jesus Christ, but rather, as in all other instances, a God of man's own imagination. Our knowledge of Allah comes from the Koran, which came through Muhammad. Muhammad, like Buddha and unlike Jesus Christ, did not claim deity. He taught that he was only the prophet of Allah. The picture of God which comes through to us in the pages of the Koran is of one who is totally removed from men, one who is capricious in all of His acts, responsible for evil as well as for good, and certainly not the God who "so loved the world that He gave His only begotten Son, that whosoever believeth in Him should not perish but have everlasting life." It is this totally distant concept of God that makes the idea of the Incarnation utterly inconceivable to the Muslim. How could their god, so majestic and beyond, have contact with mortal man in sin and misery? The death of God the Son on the cross is likewise inconceivable to a Muslim, since this would mean God was defeated by His creatures, an impossibility to them.

The Jewish concept of God is closest of all to the Christian. Isn't the God whom they worship the God of the Old Testament, which we accept? Surely we can get together on this!

Again, however, closer examination shows that the Jews would not admit their God was the Father of Jesus Christ. In fact, it was this very issue that precipitated such bitter controversy in our Lord's time. God we accept, they said to Christ, but we do not accept You because as a man you make yourself God, which is blasphemy.

In a conversation with the Jews, our Lord discussed this question. "God is our Father," they said. Jesus said to them, "If God were your Father, ye would love Me, for I proceeded forth and came from God. . . . He that is of God heareth God's words: ye therefore hear them not because ye are not of God" (John 8:42-47). In even stronger words He says, "Ye are of your father the devil" (v. 44).

Here, in our Lord's own words, we have the clue as to what our attitude should be toward those who are sincerely seeking "God." If they are seeking the true God, their sincerity will be evidenced by the fact that they will receive Christ when they hear about Him. Missionary history has numerous examples of those who have been following other gods or an unknown god but who have responded when presented with the truth about the Lord Jesus Christ. They have immediately realized that He is the true God, whom they have been seeking.

Scripture is clear throughout the Old Testament and in the New that worship of gods other than the true God originates with the devil. "And they shall no more offer their sacrifices unto devils" (Lev. 17:1), and "But I say, that the things which the Gentiles sacrifice, they sacrifice to demons, and not to God" (I Cor. 10:20, marg.).

Of the great religious leaders of the world, Christ alone claims deity. It really doesn't matter what one thinks of Muhammad, Buddha, or Confucius as individuals. Their followers emphasize their *teachings*. Not so with Christ. He made *Himself* the focal point of His teaching. The central question He put to His listeners was, "Whom do you say that *I* am?" When asked what doing the works of God involved, Jesus replied, "This is the work of God, that ye believe on Him whom He hath sent" (John 6:29).

On the question of who and what God is, the nature of salvation and how it is obtained, it is clear that Christianity differs radically from other world religions. We live in an age in which tolerance is a key word. Tolerance, however, must be clearly understood. (Truth, by its very nature, is intolerant of error.) If two plus two is four, the total cannot at the same time be 23. But one is not regarded as intolerant because he disagrees with *this* answer and maintains that the only correct answer is *four*.

The same principle applies in religious matters. One must be tolerant of other points of view and respect their right to be held and heard. He cannot, however, be forced in the name of tolerance to agree that all points of view, including those that are mutually contradictory, are equally valid. Such a position is nonsense.

It is not true that "it doesn't matter what you believe as long as you believe it." Hitler's slaughter of five million Jews was based on a sincere view of race supremacy, but he was desperately wrong. What we believe must be true in order to be real. Jesus said, "I am the Way, the Truth and the Life. No man cometh unto the Father but by Me" (John 14:6). There are many ways to Christ, but if we are to know the true and living God in personal experience, it must be through Christ, the only Way to God.

CHAPTER 12

IS CHRISTIAN
EXPERIENCE VALID?

"YOU COULD GET the same response from that table lamp if you believed it possessed the same attributes as your God," said the young law student. This articulate skeptic was telling me what thousands feel—that Christian experience is completely personal and subjective, and has no objective, eternal, and universal validity.

The premise behind this notion is that the mind is capable of infinite rationalization. Belief in God is seen as mere wish-fulfillment. In adults, it is a throw-back to our need for a father-image.

The assumption, whether expressed or not, is that Christianity is for emotional cripples who can't make it through life without a crutch.

It is claimed that Christian conversion is a psychologically induced experience brought about by "brainwashing" as used by both Fascists and Communists. An evangelist is just a master of psychological manipulation. After pounding away at an audience, people become putty in his hands. He can get them to do anything if he asks for a "decision" at the right time and in the right way.

Some go further. Christian experience, they

claim, is sometimes positively harmful. More than one student has been packed off to a psychiatrist by unbelieving parents after he has come to personal faith in Christ. "Look at all the religious nuts in mental asylums. It's their religion that put them there." Those who feel this way have succumbed to the "common-factor fallacy" pointed out by Anthony Standen. He tells of a man who got drunk each Monday on whiskey and soda water; on Tuesday he got drunk on brandy and soda water; and on Wednesday on gin and soda water. What caused the drunkenness? Obviously the common factor, soda water![1]

For many, the Church is thought of as the last stop on the train before being institutionalized. A careful scrutiny of a truly disoriented person, however, would reveal imbalance and unreality in other areas as well as in his religious life. It is actually a credit to the Church that she is willing to offer help to these people. On the other hand, some mental disturbances have spiritual roots. As *these* people come into a right relationship with God through Jesus Christ they find immediate release and healing.

So strong is the prejudice in some quarters against the validity of Christian experience that academic degrees have been denied. A friend, studying in one of our best known universities, was denied a Ph.D. degree in social science. He was told, "Believing what you do about God, you are by definition crazy."

It is suggested by some skeptics that all Christian experience can be explained on the basis of conditioned reflexes. This thinking has its roots in experiments by Pavlov, the famous Russian scien-

---

[1]*Standen.* Op. cit., p. 25.

tist. He placed measuring devices in a dog's mouth and stomach to determine the production of digestive juices. Then he would bring food to the dog and at the same time ring a bell. After doing this repeatedly over a period of time, Pavlov rang the bell without producing the food and the dog salivated as usual. The inference drawn is that by such repeated conditioning, the mind can be made to produce desired physical reactions. It is on this basis that we can explain all political, social, and religious conversions, say the proponents of this view.

These are serious, far-reaching charges. Some of them have an air of plausibility. Is Christian experience valid?

At the outset, we must concede the possibility of manipulating human emotions in some circumstances. And we would have to admit that some evangelists consciously or unconsciously play on the emotions of their audiences with deathbed stories, histrionic performances, and other devices. Our Lord, in the parable of the sower, implicitly warns against merely stirring the emotions in evangelism. He describes those who have received the seed of the Word into stony places as those that have heard the Word and received it with joy but who have no roots in themselves. They endure until tribulation and persecution come, and then they are "soon offended." All of us have known people who have made what appears to be a tremendous response to the Gospel, only to fall by the wayside. Often this happens when they learn that it "costs" something to be a Christian and are not prepared to pay the price. Their emotions are stirred but their wills had not been bent to obey the Lord.

Dr. Orville S. Walters, Director of Student

Health at the University of Illinois, a Christian psychiatrist, has pointed out that the will is like a cart pulled by two horses, the emotions and the intellect. With some people the will is reached more quickly through the emotions. With others it is reached through the mind. But in every case there is no genuine conversion unless the will has been involved.[2]

Realizing these potentialities for manipulating emotions, even unconsciously, all who are involved in evangelistic work, whether with children or with adults, must eliminate, so far as is humanly possible, factors and techniques which could produce these abortive results. But to attempt to explain *all* Christian experience on a psychological basis does not fit the facts. In passing, it is well to observe a principle that applies here as well as in other areas, i.e., to describe something is not the same thing as explaining it. To be sure, Christian experience can be described psychologically, but this does not explain *why* it happens nor negate its reality.

One evidence that Christianity is true is the reality of the experience of those who embrace Jesus Christ. One of the challenges a Christian throws out to skeptics is, "Taste and see that the Lord is good" (Ps. 34:8). Verify for yourself, in the laboratory of life, the hypothesis that Jesus Christ is the living Son of God. The reality of Christian experience is evidence of the validity of Christianity.

What of the objections that Christian experience is merely a conditioned reflex? First we must ask, as Dr. D. Martyn Lloyd-Jones does in answering the influential book, *Battle for the Mind*, by William Sargant, whether the comparison between

---

[2]*Walters, Orville S.* You Can Win Others. *Winona Lake, Ind.: Light and Life Press, 1950.*

men and animals is a strictly legitimate one. Man has reason and a critical faculty, and has powers of self-analysis, self-contemplation, and self-criticism which make him quite different from animals. "In other words, the comparison is only valid at times (like war) when what differentiates man has been knocked out of action and a man, because of terrible stress, has been reduced for the time being to a level of an animal."[3]

Second, if we are only creatures of conditioned reflexes, then this must also explain acts of great heroism and self-sacrifice in which man has taken pride. Such acts must be nothing but responses to a given stimulus at a given point. Taken to its logical conclusion, a deterministic view of human behavior eliminates moral responsibility. The little girl who said, "It ain't my fault, it's my glands," was right. It is significant, however, that those holding a deterministic point of view philosophically tend to operate on a different basis in daily life: like anyone else, they want a wallet stealer arrested promptly!

We cannot explain Christian experience on a conditioned reflex basis, however. Since thousands reared in Christian homes unfortunately never become Christians, the fact that many others really trust Christ cannot be explained exclusively on the basis of background. Though personal faith in Christ is the only door to becoming a Christian, the roads that lead to that door are almost as many as the number who enter it. I have known persons who became Christians *the first time* they heard the Gospel. It is significant, by contrast, that in political brainwashing, as with Pavlov's experi-

---

[3]*Lloyd-Jones, D. Martyn.* Conversions: Psychological or Spiritual, *p. 13. Chicago: Inter-Varsity Press, 1959.*

ments, the stimulus must be applied repeatedly for some time in order to get the desired result.

Those who have become Christians, out of every conceivable religious background and out of no background at all, testify uniformly to an experience through personal commitment to Jesus Christ. The evidence of their changed lives testifies to the reality of the experience. This result cannot be gained from a bridge lamp by positive thinking. If positive thinking were the answer to everything, we would have no problems. As a matter of fact, the law student previously referred to committed his life to Christ in the course of the week's lectures that followed.

But how do we Christians know that we are not victims of autohypnosis? How do we know we are not just whistling in the dark? Subjective experience as such does not prove anything. Many have claimed experiences the reality of which we may legitimately question. There must be more than experience on which to base our conviction, or we could be in difficulty.

For instance, suppose a man with a fried egg over his left ear came through the door of your church. "Oh," he glows, "this egg really gives me joy, peace, purpose in life, forgiveness of sins, and strength for living!" What would you say to him? You can't tell him he hasn't experienced these things. One of the powers of personal testimony is that it can't be argued. The blind man mentioned in John 9 couldn't answer many of the questions put to him, but he was sure of the fact that now he could see. His testimony was eloquent in its power.

But we could ask several questions of our friend with the fried egg. These are questions we Christians must also be prepared to *answer*.

First, who else has had the same experience with

the fried egg? Presumably our friend would be hard put to produce others. The late Harry Ironside was preaching, some years ago, when a heckler shouted, "Atheism has done more for the world than Christianity!" "Very well," said Ironside, "tomorrow night you bring a hundred men whose lives have been changed for the better by atheism, and I'll bring a hundred who have been transformed by Christ." Needless to say, his heckler friend did not appear the next night. With Christianity, there are hundreds from every race, every country, and every walk of life who bear testimony to an experience through Jesus Christ.

Secondly, we should ask our friend with the fried egg, What objective reality outside of himself is his internal subjective experience tied to? How does he *know* he is not a victim of autohypnosis? Of course he will have nothing to say. In Christianity our personal subjective experience is tied into the objective historical fact of the resurrection of Christ. If Christ had not risen from the dead we would not experience Him. It's because He rose from the dead and is living today that we can actually know Him.

Christian experience is not induced by belief in unrealities. It is not like the fraternity boy who died of fright when tied to a railroad track one night during hazing. He was told that a train would be coming in five minutes. He was not told that the train would pass on a parallel track. He thought there was only one track. When he heard the train approaching he suffered heart failure. With Christianity, nothing happens if there is "no one out there."

Because Christ is really "there," all the possibilities of His life within us are realizable. It is only half the story when we sing, "He lives within my heart." The other crucial half is that we know He lives because He rose from the dead *in history*. Our personal subjective experience is based on objective historical *fact*.

In commenting on the truth that people, in suffering, speak of drawing upon power outside themselves, J. B. Phillips says, "I know perfectly well that I am merely describing subjective phenomena. But the whole point is that when I have observed results in *objective* phenomena—courage, faith, hope, joy, and patience, for instance—and these qualities are very readily observed. The man who wants everything proved by scientific means is quite right in his insistence on 'laboratory conditions' if he is investigating, shall we say, water-divining, clairvoyance, or telekinesis. But there can be no such thing as 'laboratory conditions' for investigating the realm of the human spirit unless it can be seen that the 'laboratory conditions' are in fact human life itself. A man can only exhibit objectively a change in his own disposition, a faith which directs his life—*in the actual business of living*."[4]

It is in these objective results in personal life that we see some of the dynamic relevance of Christ. He meets man in his deepest needs.

Christ gives purpose and direction to life. "I am the Light of the world," He says. "He that followeth Me shall not walk in darkness, but shall have the Light of life" (John 8:12). Many are in the dark about the purpose of life in general and about their own lives in particular. They are groping around the room of life looking for the light switch. Anyone who has ever been in a dark, unfamiliar room knows this feeling of insecurity. When the

---

[4]*Phillips.* Op. cit., *pp. 22, 23.*

light goes on, however, a feeling of security results. And so it is when one steps from darkness to the light of life in Christ.

God in Christ gives our lives cosmic purpose, tying them in with His purpose for history and eternity. A Christian lives not only for time, but for eternity. Even routine is transformed as we live the whole of our lives in God's purpose and obey the admonition, "Whether, therefore, ye eat or drink, or whatsoever ye do, do all to the glory of God" (I Cor. 10:31). This purpose embraces every aspect of life. It is also an unending, eternal purpose. Undoubtedly a non-Christian has such temporary purposes as family, career, and money that give limited satisfaction. But these, at best, are transient and may fail with a change in circumstances.

To an age in which life has been described as meaningless and absurd by existentialist philosophers, nothing could have more power and meaning than this verifiable claim of Christ.

The late Carl Gustav Jung said, "The central neurosis of our time is emptiness." When we do not have money, fame, success, power, and other externals, we think we'll achieve final happiness after we attain them. Many testify to the disillusionment experienced when these have been achieved and the realization sets in that one is still the same miserable person. The human spirit can never be satisfied "by bread alone"—by material things. We have been made for God and can never find rest until we rest in Him.

An automobile, however shiny, high-powered, and full of equipment, will not run on water. It was made to run *only* on gasoline. So man can find fulfillment only in God. He was made this way by God Himself. Christian experience offers this fulfillment in a personal relationship to Christ. He said, "I am the Bread of life: he that cometh to Me shall never hunger and he that believeth on Me shall never thirst" (John 6:35). When one experiences Christ, he comes to an inner contentment, joy, and spiritual refreshment which enables him to transcend circumstances. It was this reality that enabled Paul to say, "I have learned, in whatsoever state I am, therewith to be content" (Phil. 4:11). This supernatural reality enables a Christian to rejoice in the middle of difficult circumstances.

"Peace in our time" expresses the longing of all men as they view the international scene. We hope against hope that the current brush-fire wars will not erupt into a large-scale conflict.

Peace is the quest of every human heart. If it could be bought, people would pay millions for it. The skyrocketing sales of books dealing with peace of mind and soul testify that they have touched a resonant chord in the lives of millions. Psychiatrists' offices are jammed.

Jesus says, "Come unto Me, all ye that labor and are heavy laden, and I will give you rest" (Matt. 11:28). Christ alone gives peace that passes understanding, a peace the world cannot give or take away. It is very moving to hear the testimony of those who have restlessly searched for years and have finally found peace in Christ. The current rise in narcotic addiction, alcoholism, and sex obsession are vain hopes of gaining the peace which is in Christ alone. "He is our peace" (Eph. 2:14).

Today's society is experiencing a profound power failure—a moral power failure. Parents know what is right for themselves and their children, but for lack of backbone they find it easier to go along with the crowd. Children readily pick up this attitude. The result is rapid deterioration of the moral fabric of society. Merely to give good advice to either the old or young is like putting iodine on cancer. What is needed is radical *power*. Christianity is not the putting of a new suit on a man, but the putting of a new man into the suit. Jesus Christ said, "I am come that they might have life, and that they might have it more abundantly" (John 10:10). He offers us His power. Not only is there power and freedom from things like alcohol and narcotics, but power to forgive those who have wronged us, to resist temptation, and to love the unlovely. Twice-born men have new appetites, new desires, new loves. They are, in fact, "new creatures" (II Cor. 5:17). Salvation is a literal coming from death to spiritual life.

Christian experience solves the guilt problem. Every normal person feels guilt. A guilt complex is an *irrational* feeling that has no basis in fact. But guilt felt over something done wrongly, in violation of an inherent moral law, is *normal*. The absence of any guilt feeling is abnormal. A person who feels nothing after deliberately killing or hurting an innocent person is abnormal. Guilt must not be rationalized away. In Christ, there is an objective basis for forgiveness. Christ died for our sins; the sentence of death that belonged to us has been taken by Him. "There is therefore no condemnation to them which are in Christ Jesus" (Rom. 8:1). Forgiveness at the personal level is a reality.

Christianity speaks to man's loneliness, so characteristic of modern society. It is ironic that in a period of population explosion man is more lonely than ever. Christ is the Good Shepherd (John 10:14) who will never leave us nor forsake us. And He introduces us into a worldwide family and a fellowship closer than a blood-relationship with an unbeliever."[5]

Finally, in recognizing the validity of Christian experience we should realize that a psychological description of it is valid as far as it goes. But it is only a *description*, not a *cause*. A man who is converted has a new spiritual life within him. This new life will thoroughly affect his entire personality. One part of man's nature cannot be altered without affecting the rest of him.

Man's brain and nervous system may be analyzed in the same way as his heart and kidneys. The body and spirit are inextricably intertwined. Man is this totality. He is not merely a spirit encased in a body. On the other hand, his mind is a reality. The mechanical and spiritual aspects of life are complementary. Dr. Donald M. MacKay puts it very helpfully:

"One familiar illustration is that of the use of lamps to signal from ships at sea. When a man sends a message from ship to shore, in one sense all that is coming from the ship is a series of flashes of light, but the trained sailor who sits on the shore watching this light says, 'I see a message ordering so-and-so to proceed somewhere,' or 'Look, they're in trouble!' Why does he say this? All he has seen is 'nothing but' flashes of light. The whole pattern of activity can be correctly labeled thus by a physicist, and described so completely that he is able to reproduce at any time exactly what the man on shore saw. He does not add 'the message' as a kind of 'extra' at the end of his description, and it would clearly be silly to say he is 'leaving out the mes-

[5]*For an expansion of these experiences and their relevancy to life, see the author's* How to Give Away Your Faith, *pp. 83 ff. Chicago: Inter-Varsity Press, 1966.*

sage' as if it were very wrong of him to do so. What he has done is to choose one way of approaching a complex unity, namely the sending-of-a-message-from-ship-to-shore, one aspect of which is a purely physical allowing of complete description in such terms as the wave lengths of the light and the time-pattern. On the other hand, if he reads it also as a message, it is not as if he had found something mysterious, as well as the flashing, going on. Instead he has discovered that the whole thing, when he allows it to strike him in a different way, can be *read* and can also make sense in nonphysical terms. The message here is related to the flashing of light, not as an effect is to a cause, but rather as one aspect of a complex unity is related to another aspect.

"Take another illustration. Two mathematicians start arguing about a problem in geometry. With a piece of chalk, they make a pattern of dots and lines on the board, and the fun waxes fast and furious. Can we imagine some nonmathematician coming in and saying, in amazement, 'I can't see what you're arguing about—there's nothing there but chalk'? Once again this would illustrate what I like to call the fallacy of 'nothing-buttery'—the idea that because, in one sense, at one level, or viewed from one angle, there is nothing there but chalk, therefore it is unnecessary . . . to talk about what is there in any other terms. Again, if the mathematicians protest, 'But there is a geometrical figure there; we are talking about these angles,' they are not suggesting that the other man's eyes are failing to detect something that they are seeing on the board. Both of them are responding to exactly the same light waves. It is not that the mathematicians have a sixth sense or anything queer that enables them to receive from the board some invisible emanations that the other fellow is not receiving. The point is that, as a result of a different attitude to what is there, they have power to see in it, or, if you like, to abstract from it, an aspect or significance which the other misses. Of course, in this case he can be trained to discover it. There is no great difficulty in their eventually coming to agreement, and he then realizes that the geometrical pattern is related to the chalk on the board, not indeed as effect is to a cause, but in a still more intimate way.

"I want to clarify this alternative to 'a cause and effect,' because it bears on questions that are often raised about the 'causation' of bodily action by mental activity. If an argument were to come up as to whether the light causes the message or the message causes the light, whether the chalk-distribution causes the geometrical figure or the geometrical figure causes the chalk-distribution, we would see at once that the word 'cause,' in the scientific sense, is the wrong one here. Causality in science is a relationship between two events or sets of events, the cause and the effect. Here we have not two events or situations, but one. You cannot have the flashing of the light without the message: they are one set of events. You cannot have the chalk-distribution without there being, at the same time, the figure on the board. On the other hand, the two do have a certain kind of independence. It would be possible to reproduce the same message or figure in a quite different embodiment—in ink or pencil, for example. It is for this reason that I prefer to say that the one 'embodies' the other."[6]

As Christians, we need not fear psychological de-

[6]*MacKay, Donald M.* Christianity in a Mechanistic Universe, *pp. 57-59. London: Inter-Varsity Fellowship, 1965.*

scriptions of Christian experience. They are not explanations. The fact that some Christian experiences can be produced by other means is a warning against the temptation to manipulate human personality. The fact that solid Christian experience is also sound mental health is an asset rather than a detriment, and is an evidence of the Gospel's validity.